My Everything

My Everything

The Parent I Want to Be,
The Children I Hope to Raise

EINAT NATHAN

hachette
BOOKS

NEW YORK

Hachette Go, an imprint of Hachette Books
Hachette Book Group
1290 Avenue of the Americas
New York, NY 10104
HachetteGo.com
Facebook.com/HachetteGo
Instagram.com/HachetteGo

First Edition: April 2021
Hachette Books is a division of Hachette Book Group, Inc.

The Hachette Go and Hachette Books name and logos are trademarks of
Hachette Book Group, Inc.

The publisher is not responsible for websites (or their content) that are not
owned by the publisher.

Print book interior design by Linda Mark

Library of Congress Control Number: 2020950742

ISBNs: 978-0-306-92404-0 (hardcover), 978-0-306-92405-7 (e-book)

Printed in the United States of America

LSC-C

Printing 1, 2021

*Dedicated to my late mother, Miriam, that no day goes by
without the deepest yearn for her words, her smile, and her touch*

Contents

one

Parenthood: The True Story

THE STORY OF HOW WE BECOME PARENTS, THE PARENTS we are and the parents we will be in the future, is a story that's rewritten every day and every moment. It's a story about falling in love and about love itself, about communication and ego, about fear and hardship, about old pains we've forgotten and new ones that are created along the way. It's a story about bravery and modesty, imperfection, harmony and disharmony, but, most of all, it's a story that has several narrators and different points of view.

Drawing from thousands of encounters with parents, my own personal parenting experience, and the professional knowledge I have accumulated, I write here about the complicated tale of parenthood as I see it. The lessons my children teach me are written in my life's story and are presented to you here following my belief that this is how we should be talking about parenthood today.

Children come into the world without any operating manuals. Just as we wouldn't dream of feeding them every other day or of changing their diapers only when we feel like it, we cannot set out on the journey of parenthood without understanding what our children need on the emotional level in order to evolve into complete human beings. That's why we often find ourselves quite lost when standing in front of the parenting bookshelf, succumbing to new techniques that promise us a child who will sleep through the night, excel at AP classes, and send us flowers every week along with a note thanking us for all that we do for him. At the same time, we are less attentive to the intuitive voice inside us and too attentive to our anxieties and other parents on the playground. We don't have enough fun, we're often struggling, exhausted and angry, and the whole thing is wrapped up in a nice package of guilt, because we feel we're never doing enough.

Our most significant challenge as parents is to try to expand the way we automatically interpret things and to rethink our reactions: "That girl wakes up every morning just to drive me crazy," "He's testing me," "She's being manipulative," "He's doing it on purpose," "They'll kill each other if we don't step in," and countless other phrases we write in our narrative. Then we respond—we put out the fires they light, get annoyed when they're annoying, enjoy them when they're cute or cooperative, and generally find ourselves dependent on them and their behaviors. We are not really in control. Many things actually are beyond our control, but we *can* control the relationships at home.

I believe in taking control of the familial environment. I believe in improving relationships. I believe in parental intuition and good intentions. I believe that sometimes it's enough to think differently or interpret things in a different way to make things better and include more moments of happiness in the story we write.

When you read my words, I hope you understand your own stories better. The most important discussion about parenthood is not related to techniques or tips, or to authority, rules, or boundaries, either. The most important thing about talking parenthood is discussing relationships. The parent-child relationship is not an equal relationship, but a relationship where the value of equality is present. It's a relationship in which we have to figure out the nature of our role (and yes, it is a role), understand what our children are telling us even when they're not saying anything, know what is really required—and no, it isn't necessarily to be tougher or to set more boundaries. Above all, it's about observing the work from the viewpoint of the relationship between us and them, through the understanding of how significant we are to them, taking into consideration the life skills we would want to give them and their self-esteem, which is in our hands. This relationship needs to survive growing, failing, becoming an adult, learning, and disagreeing, and must provide children with what they need to face the challenges of living in the jungle out there—the difficulties, the social relations, the formation of their identity, the tasks of life. Ultimately, when there's a good relationship to lean on, we too become stronger.

Parenthood is like a bungee jump. It's scary and fun, it makes you fly and flings you down, and as the wind blows in your face between heaven and earth after you've dared to take that leap, there are a few moments of unparalleled exhilaration and joy. Remember that you're tied by a lifeline: your kids are the best anchor you can have for a jump like that. They're the ones who keep us in the parental role that requires so much courage, and they're the only ones who make these magical moments possible. So hold on tight and take a deep breath. We're off.

— two —

Children and Silence
Don't Go Together

W E WERE ON OUR WAY TO THE DELIVERY ROOM, AN excited and loving couple pregnant with twin boys in the thirty-ninth week. In a few hours we would be a family. Over the past few months we had done everything we were supposed to: we ordered all the baby equipment and moved from our one-bedroom urban pad right above a singles-packed sandwich bar to a quiet neighborhood where people walked around with strollers.

I entered the monitoring room alone, while Yuval waited outside. With twins, it's always hard to find the heartbeat at first, but I knew where they were each nestled in my body—the three of us had been together for many months. The one on the right was very active; his brother was quieter, but no less present. I told the midwife where to look for them and advised that she begin with the left one: "You always find his heartbeat first, he's more patient," I joked. "His brother is another story."

I remember her having some trouble for a few minutes, and I thought to myself that she was probably fresh out of nursing school.

"Are you here alone or is there someone with you?" she asked, and then stepped outside to get Yuval, knowing before we did that these were the final seconds before our universe collapsed.

Yuval came in with a worried expression. The midwife came right after him, accompanied by a doctor, and they both explained very cautiously that they would need to do an ultrasound to locate the heartbeats. Yuval held my hand as he had in every previous ultrasound. The doctor looked at the screen, laid down the probe, and told us that the life within me had ended.

It was my second pregnancy. The first had ended after twenty-two weeks. We had felt so grief-stricken and doomed, we experienced the tremendous loss in all its intensity. Four months after we parted with our eldest daughter, I felt as if God was compensating me when I saw the two pulses on the monitor. There was poetic justice in those two that had come to console my womb: I would have two children, one for the loss I experienced, and the other as a sibling. There must be some greater scheme of things after all, we thought. The pregnancy was not easy, but after we got through the amniocentesis, which marked the stage where our first pregnancy had ended, we felt we had made it. I could make babies that didn't have a scary genetic flaw. Everything was okay.

At some point, I was put on bed rest, because my tiny body couldn't handle the mass. I would stretch both arms out and feel my belly end at the tips of my fingers. I was mainly preoccupied with obsessive thoughts about getting back into my jeans after this extraterrestrial experience and yearned to get to week thirty-six, as my gynecologist had commanded, to escape the risk of early labor. I was a real bed-rest trooper. I rested and watched over the pregnancy, and it watched over me, but someone up there fell asleep on their watch.

A stillbirth is named for what it lacks; there is no baby crying, no movement. Up to week twenty-two, if something is wrong with the fetus, abortion is possible. If it happens later, the fetus usually needs to be delivered. This procedure is just like any other birthing, with a delivery room, induction, contractions. Sometimes the fetus has died in the womb because of a defect or a nuchal cord, for example, but in a high percentage of cases, as in ours, no one knows what went wrong.

How do you process something like that? The truth is, you don't. For an hour and a half, I screamed and cried with a voice I never thought could come out of me. When I felt my eyelids completely swollen from tears, I finally understood the real meaning of "the tears have all dried up." Then I realized that the hardest parts were still ahead. I had to go through childbirth and, even before that, we had to let our families know: to call my caring and loving father and Yuval's parents, who had been on "twin alert" for many days. My father arrived within half an hour. Thirty minutes later, Yuval's parents were also there. I had seen my father cry only a few times, and this was the hardest time of all.

They sat outside the delivery room in the company of excited soon-to-be grandparents, hearing more and more reports of full dilations, brave mothers, and perfect babies. When my father hugged me, all I could manage to say was "Sorry, Dad." I was sorry for the disappointment I had caused, for the pain and sadness they were feeling, for not managing to fulfill such a simple expectation: to give them grandchildren.

I must have realized that to alleviate some of their pain I would have to be strong, glue the pieces of myself back together.

For my own sake, for Yuval's sake, and for them. That was when dark humor entered the delivery room. I don't remember exactly what I said, but we laughed a lot. We laughed and cried. And right there, in the midst of the hysterical laughter and painful sobbing, I began to realize that we were going to be all right, that I was strong enough to look inside and find a few scraps of joy for myself and for the people I loved most. I would be okay, and then they would be okay.

Eighteen hours later, I pushed, and my first son was out. I was sure the one on the right would have been first; inside, he had the nature of a firstborn. He must have let his brother go before him, I thought. A few minutes later, the one on the right joined him. The medical staff urged me to hold them, to say goodbye and give them one last kiss. One of the midwives told me how beautiful they were, my dead babies, and how important it was to the grieving process to say goodbye. But if I saw them, I would go mad. I just knew, deep inside, that what little life I had left in me in that delivery room would not be mine if I held my dead children. "What kind of mother doesn't want to say goodbye to her kids?" I wondered, while they stitched me up. Everything ached and felt blurry, but the realization that I had to save myself was very clear. Just like Lot's wife, I knew I couldn't look or I'd turn into a pillar of salt. So, to survive, I chose to be a mother who leaves behind her dead children. On March 7, 1999, in delivery room number 6, I chose life.

That year, the Ministry of Health had prohibited the use of drugs that dry up breast milk. At home, I found myself standing in the shower, my body battered, my stitches aching, and milk dripping from my breasts. It was a terrible shower. I was so looking forward to that first shower at home, but no one had prepared me for that cruel moment when breast milk would seep out of me, reminding me that I had no one to feed. I sat down on the shower floor, with the water running over me, the milk leaking, and the tears. The delivery was behind me, but the rest of my life was still ahead of me.

"Congratulations!" cried the grocer, and the hairdresser, and the nice lady next door, and all the other good people who were ignorant of what had happened in our lives, and I was mostly upset by the fact that my response to this routine greeting would make them so uncomfortable. I would check myself in the mirror and head out into the street, looking completely intact on the outside but broken and shattered on the inside. I would watch the passersby and wonder who was as torn up inside as I was. It was such a lie, this camouflage of clothes, smiles, makeup, and a particular kind of walk. If only all the broken people were somehow marked with little signs so that we could be more careful with them, maybe smile at them a little more, not pity them, just offer a little consolation.

After two weeks at home, it became clear. Life is short—Yuval and I chose happiness. We clung to our love for one another. We flew to New York because it was far away, far from the kind people's pitying looks. Maybe there we would manage to stop feeling sorry for ourselves and remind ourselves of the most important thing of all: we could pull through this, our togetherness could bring us great happiness, and happiness is a choice we make every day.

For three weeks we walked around New York City, spending money and loving. It did the trick. On March 9 a year later, Eyal was born, seven pounds and three ounces of life. And when I held him for the first time, pulsing and mewling in my arms, I said goodbye to them, too. I held them in my heart. I cried with the excitement of this meeting and cried with the sorrow of the other parting; I cried for what I had won and cried for what I had lost; and most of all I cried because he was crying, and what a joy it was to hear the wailing of a baby in the delivery room.

The term *stillbirth* is inaccurate. In the absence of the baby's crying, the silence is thunderous, not still. Inside the soul of the mother who is mourning the dream that has died, the empty arms, and the expectation of a meeting that will never take place, there is anything but stillness. I don't know why it happened to me, but I do know what happened as a result of it happening to me. I know that it forged a new alliance in my relationship with my husband and nurtured a new love, a love that endured one of the greatest blows life can deal a twenty-eight-year-old couple.

Today I know that we gained life, learned a sense of proportion, learned faith and will. The tragedy we suffered reared the parents we are today. I know that those three children who died in my womb made me a different mother to my five children. I know that because of them I handle the daily difficulties of motherhood and feel grateful for any "ordinary" challenge life throws my way. I know I have been blessed with the privilege of truly appreciating a baby's crying, children's crying, and crying in general, because I have been to a place where babies don't cry.

That experience has shifted to a different place inside me. A significant place that reminds me to be content with my share, a distant, painful place that misses those babies I never met but that is at the same time intact and closed. Sometimes, when I see a mother pushing a twins' stroller, I remember my shattered dream, and I hug myself from inside, and then when I get home I put on some really loud music and dance in the kitchen with my kids. Because children and silence don't go together.

three

Your Child Is Not
Your Calling Card

A LITTLE BOY IN STARRED PAJAMAS LIES CURLED UP IN bed, his mind ensconced in pleasant dreams, his face as serene as an angel's. Finally, all is quiet. They're so beautiful when they're asleep. For just one second, I feel like a good mother. I'm full of warmth and compassion and total empathy for them and their needs.

Kids are pure joy, no doubt in my heart about that, but I also have no doubt about the gap that appears between fantasy and reality the moment they open their eyes. After all, they go on and on about things, making me want to die of boredom; they embarrass me, especially in public places or around people whose opinions really matter to me; they fight everywhere and at any given opportunity; they eat constantly and create an endless mess and piles of laundry. And that's just when things are actually okay, knock on wood, when they're not sick or anxious or dealing with social issues or problems at school or coming home drunk.

And me, what kind of mother am I? Mainly a "not enough" mother. I'm not patient enough, I don't take enough interest, don't spend enough time at the playground, don't give them enough treatments against lice; I'm not helping enough with homework, not solving-fifty-problems-at-once-enough. And also, sometimes I'm bored, frustrated, grumpy, tired, confused, angry, and helpless.

But here's a newsflash: my kids are not my calling card, and that is actually the most challenging thing to understand.

Our kids are the greatest and most important creation we've brought into this world. We teach them almost everything—how to talk, eat, behave, and accept authority. No wonder we get confused and think they are our calling cards. But if that's how we see them, once they mess up, embarrass us, or disappoint us, we feel hurt. And when we feel hurt, we're focusing on ourselves. And when we're focusing on ourselves, we're not free to fulfill our parental duty.

Kids are the best psychotherapy available to a conscious person. They take us back to the landscapes of our own painful and thrilling childhoods, they are always the first to identify our weak spots, but most of all they are a deep mirror that confronts us with the fact that we never were and never will be perfect. Our fantasies may have come true while we planned our wedding or furnished our home, but the kids leave us with the day-to-day, with the greatest lesson life has to offer. This is a lesson that requires us to pack up our ego and leave it at the door, to be present as human beings with good intentions and plenty of mistakes, to accept ourselves unconditionally and then to accept the other—the kids—unconditionally.

So if you sometimes feel you're "not enough," you should know that this is actually the kind of feeling the good parents have. Part of being a good parent is accepting the fact that sometimes you are not good enough. It's actually the moments in which we manage to abide in the experience of frustration or imperfection that allow us to change our way or, alternatively, accept ourselves as imperfect. Our children get to see the model of a parent who brings herself into the relationship, whole but not necessarily perfect, who sees the needs of her children but is not necessarily able to satisfy them all. And there, in the space between the parent who wishes to be perfect but isn't and the child whose process of growing is a continuum of imperfect experiences, a third entity grows—the relationship. It is only when we surrender the role of educators, authority figures, those who punish, know everything, and have it easy that we can meet our children in an experience of equal worth (not equal rights—the two shouldn't be confused).

Our children were not born to make us happy or proud or pleased with ourselves. The goal is to get through raising them with all the chaos they bring into our lives and to be good enough parents to them; not perfect ones, but not sad or worried ones either. Moderately frustrated but sufficiently fun-filled, listening and attentive to their needs but also to our own needs sometimes, and most of all wholly willing to be there even when it's not the exact picture we painted in our fantasies.

It's only by accepting ourselves as imperfect-but-getting-better that we can gradually learn to worry less about our children and accept them as imperfect-but-learning, falling over but getting up, nice and grumpy, happy and demanding, little people, short and sometimes annoying, who carry the burden of our parenthood—a weight that is the role of *our* lifetime.

four

When We Worry, We Miss Out

I FLIP THROUGH AN OLD PHOTO ALBUM CONTAINING photos from a different house, where I was a mother to three small children, the oldest of whom was five. More than ten years separate the mother I am today from that girl-mother I was back then, and now, looking through the photos, my eyes are flooded with tears of sorrow. Sorrow for my old self: so young, exhausted, blind to the beauty of magical moments, enduring through a mess of laundry and toy parts, functional but far from happy, and above all—anxious. The old me looks back at me from the photos—me and the loneliness of being a mother to small children.

I'm sure that anyone who looks at the family unit we were back then wouldn't understand what I'm talking about. But that's just the thing—my anxiety was subterranean, toxic, present 24/7, a sort of uneasiness that was lodged in the space between the diaphragm and throat and that sounded more or less like this: He's playing alone, am I supposed to leave him or join in? He's asleep now, and it's not nap time, should I wake him? Is something wrong? He doesn't point to things he wants. Children his age already use their index fingers. I'm not going to stress, but I will start pointing at things. Yes, this week I'll point plenty and he'll learn. Why isn't this breastfeeding working, for crying out loud? She feeds for five minutes and then falls asleep and whoever steps into the house makes the regular "boob out again?" joke. I'll try to make her wait a little, yes, I saw a friend who did it, no sweat. "Just let her wait," she said, "for at least two hours. Hold her some of the time, play a little." It's been twenty minutes and my breast is out again. Anxious. Why does he watch so much TV? Why, you ask yourself? Cause you're a crappy mom, that's why. Well, I'll use the time to tidy up a bit, do the laundry. Do they actually need fresh pajamas every day? Other people's kids look so neat and tidy. Why does he keep falling over? Maybe I should take him to the doctor?

While these disturbing thoughts ran through my head, I went on playing with them, tying the umpteenth ponytail, pureeing the soup I made, and singing too—wracking my brain to remember a good kids' song, but nothing would come to mind. And the soup went to the trash again because he wasn't hungry just then, or she didn't like it, or something was wrong.

When I decided to study parental counseling, right after Eyal was born, it wasn't to acquire a profession but to heal myself of that anxiety. If I keep myself busy with the techniques of good parenting, I might actually manage to become a good enough mother, I thought to myself. Everything I learned made sense and made me think and think some more, but it didn't take away the guilt or improve the daily routine. I kept on feeling like an actress in a play called "The Good Mom to Wonderful Kids," but the thing is, no one came to watch the performance or applaud at the end. But gradually, my professional identity came to life and alongside it a dream: maybe in the future, someday I would manage to help mothers like me; maybe I'd be able to tell someone something that would take away some of her anxiety and make her feel just a little less inadequate. But I knew I had to help myself first.

The first step was relatively simple. I decided I wouldn't fight anxiety but do something else: I would be committed to pleasure. Tiny little pleasures, millisecond fragments. Watching them as they slept, pulling a funny face and actually thinking it's funny, singing whatever I felt like, and even enjoying being out of tune or using words I made up when I couldn't remember the lyrics. Using curse words jokingly, and sometimes not jokingly, while talking about the job of tidying up toys: "Mommy loves you, but damn those train tracks." I even started to enjoy the liberation in making self-deprecating comments about my "messed up" kids, like the time an embarrassed neighbor popped in while my son was busy throwing his cottage cheese and yelling "Snow, snow!" They didn't teach any of that at Parental Counseling School, but those fun moments became part of our daily routine and challenged that anxiety head-to-head. Pleasure vs. Anxiety, 1–0.

Anxiety is a misleading emotion. When we're worried about someone, we believe we're there for them; but in fact, the child or the situation we're anxious about is pushed aside, and instead we concentrate on ourselves. The reasonable worry, the one that keeps us vigilant, expresses itself mainly in action, in keeping our little ones safe. The problematic anxiety is the one that makes us restless, takes away our ability to be happy, and paints the present in bleak colors even when it's pleasant. There is nothing this kind of anxiety can achieve except giving a sense of moral superiority in the way we see ourselves as mothers: After all, the good mother is the one who worries. Cultural narratives have been teaching that for years.

At the base of *helicopter parenting*, the most common and overly discussed style of parenting in the past two decades, you also find a parent with plenty of good intentions and the following agenda: "I hereby undertake to protect you at all times, remove every obstacle from your path, offer shortcuts for any process, and supervise all your activities to protect you from harm. Sometimes you will make bad, even harmful decisions, but don't worry, I'll be there too. Sometimes the world will be unkind, but don't worry, I'll turn things around, soften the blow, and guide you safely to your destination—no problem."

Sound good? The problem with this attitude is that it gives us a false sense of control, whereas one of the biggest challenges of parenting is actually the ongoing process of coping with loss of control: over our time, our sleep, our dreams about who we would be, who our children are, and who we wish them to be. Most importantly—the supposed control we assume by helicoptering only serves us while harming our kids' learning and development. Because when anxiety has a life of its own, the actions we take in its service are not necessarily right for them. In the name of worry, we withhold failure from them, do their homework, move them to a kindergarten with a nicer teacher, bring an out-of-reach toy closer when they're learning to crawl, speak for them when their words are still unclear, and keep trying to feed them even if they're keeping their mouths closed.

Worrying never translates into action; it's a painful and unnecessary state of being. When we put a sandwich in their schoolbag or take them to the doctor or pick them up on time, we're *taking care* of them. Don't confuse *caring* and *worrying*: we're supposed to *take care* of all those things that actually make us parents, but please, let go of the *anxiety* that leads you to do things instead of them, remove obstacles, or unnecessarily push them in directions that only serve you and your parental pride.

Children really need a parent who will let them hit the ground when they fall, get offended by a friend, struggle to crawl and reach that rattle, leave their sandwich behind and go hungry; who will let them fall in love with someone who doesn't love them back, play the small part in the school play even though you know they're superstars. Children need parents who will release them to experience the smaller downfalls of life because they trust their children to learn and cope, knowing that even if things get hard or uncomfortable, they will know best what to do.

Children need parents whose behavior communicates "You are the biggest expert on yourself. I'm here to help and to learn about you from you." They need parents who release their control, even if it isn't easy, out of a deep understanding that they don't have the ability or the right to control anyone. They need you to forsake that rotor spinning above them and provide a space where they can take responsibility for themselves, recognize when they are tired or hungry, and feel for themselves when they've actually been offended by a friend (as opposed to *you* deciding that a friend was being mean), a space where they know that they can do it on their own.

In adolescence, this is even more important. The kind of model that a teenager needs is "Even though I'm anxious, my parent is calm." In all those places where they feel anxiety—"I'm not pretty enough," "I'll never make it," "My girlfriend will never forgive me," "I don't know what I like"—they need us to be calm, understanding, and attentive, to put things in perspective. Your teenager needs a parent who doesn't ignore the difficulties but who looks at him or her with eyes that know everything's going to be okay, eyes that might be deliberating with them but that are not confused. Eyes that are free of worry.

On the other hand, all those places where your teen is calm—that's where you should harness the worry to try to influence them: "No biggie, Mom, everyone drinks a little at parties." "So, I'm going to a party with college kids; don't worry—it's all good." "Why are you making such a big deal out of a naughty pic I sent my boyfriend?" This is where our job is to *take care* of things. To take care of being parents, to convey important messages, set boundaries, and be meaningful, and most of all to take care that we're keeping an eye on them.

So let's redefine anxiety and get rid of all those parts that concern the future ("She won't have any friends") and the past ("If only I had breastfed/hadn't breastfed/had kept her in preschool for another year"), the things that are beyond our control ("She's going to break his heart"), and the things that are just part of his or her wonderful and separate personality ("He didn't join in at the kindergarten party").

To the old Einat, the one in the photos, I just wanted to say, "Everything's going to be okay. The difficulties don't depend on anything you do or don't do. On the contrary, it will be much better if you can just relax those two wrinkles between your brows, that troubled expression, the desperate certainty that you're never going to sleep again, the desire to solve any problem and find shortcuts for them. It is not worth letting the pursuit of the perfect picture and the fantasies that were rooted in you before they were born make you miss out on the pleasure the kids bring. Look how beautiful they are, how focused they are on the here and now."

five

How to Listen to Kids

W E'D ALL LIKE TO RAISE CHILDREN WHO KNOW WHY they are sad or troubled, who make the choices that are best for themselves, who can understand themselves, accept their shortcomings, and find their way around problems in a way that strengthens them and gives them a sense of worth. This all begins with the way we listen to them. And no, I'm not talking about when they go on and on about what happened at school today or about what went on in the last episode of their favorite TV show. Our attention becomes critical when they decide to share something difficult or distressing, an unpleasant experience.

This is hard, especially for goal-directed, pragmatic types like the man I married. "What do you mean, listen to them? What good will that do?" he asks. "I figured out what the whole thing was about from the first sentence. Now let me tell him how to solve the problem; in fact, I'll put in bullet points so he understands his options. And if he needs a bit of a wakeup call, then that's what he needs. The world won't stand still every time your child speaks."

And he goes on: "All this psychobabble gives our children the feeling that whenever they experience anything hard in life, they need to stop, look inward, ask questions, and think. Come on!" He tilts his head and makes an exaggerated face that looks like the understanding expression of an annoying psychologist.

I don't fall for it. After all, I know how to listen. So I look at my man and say, "Hey, I didn't ask you to listen to the kids. You can go on giving them wakeup calls and bullet points and tell them to get on with their lives. I'll do the listening, it's totally fine. Now tell me, what's really bugging you?"

"Suddenly they all want 'a private chat with Mom'"—now he's imitating the kids—"What's up with that? Don't you realize it's making them soft? Why don't they want private chats with Dad?"

"Why do you think?" I ask.

"Because with you they get the VIP treatment. With you they are understood. You encourage them, ask them, get excited about their thoughts! That's not real life, don't you see?"

"So, are you mad because I'm not preparing them for life or because they don't want 'private chats' with you?"

"Both, okay? And I worry most about the boys. Do you really think it's right to raise them to be so sensitive? What's the point?"

As he talks, I hear so many things he's telling me about himself: I hear his pain and his worries and the good father he is despite all that testosterone. I hear and understand what he means, and I've known him long enough to know that there are some conversations that aren't supposed to end with me being right and him being the insensitive male again. Some conversations are meant to end with me saying, "I get the feeling I understand." Just like I've learned to listen to my children through their words, their behavior, and their bodies.

So, how do we teach children to listen? We listen to them very carefully, for many years, from the day they're born. We listen to their words, their behavior, and their bodies.

Listening to Tears

The tiny baby that has just joined the world is equipped with the ability to communicate only through tears: when he cries, he sends a signal to the world, and the world responds. Knowing that I sent a signal out to the universe and the universe in turn sent back what I asked for gives me a sense of assurance—I trust myself to be able to tell the universe I am hungry and trust the universe that responds to my request. Try to imagine yourself sending a signal out to the universe and having nature immediately start a process of trying to figure out what you've asked for and how to satisfy you. Sounds good, right? The immature speech organs that human beings are born with don't allow almost anything except that form of communication at first. If there's someone listening on the other side we're off to a good start.

There's a dramatic difference between a mother who gives a bottle or the breast at fixed intervals, regardless of signals or signs from the baby, and a mother who responds to the infant crying by offering the breast. The attentive mother is not the one who provides even before the tears come, nor is she the one who predicts what her baby needs. The attentive mother is the one who listens to her baby and responds with a message that says, "You and I are going to figure out together what you need right now, and I won't rest until we solve the problem. Are you hungry, tired, or colicky? You talk and I'll listen."

Listening to Pain

"I fell in the park, Daddy came running, he always watches over me, but then he looked at the scrape on my knee and the tears in my eyes and said, 'It's nothing, sweetie, nothing at all. Everything is alright.' But it wasn't alright!"

Part of the listening process for which we are responsible as parents is listening to pain, frustration, lack of success, sadness, jealousy, and many other physiological and psychological aches our children have. Instinctively, the first thing we want to tell ourselves is "It's nothing. Everything is okay." Everything is okay even though nobody played with her at school today, everything is okay even if he was teased for being fat or the teacher punished her or she fell down and scraped her knee or he really felt homesick today or someone wrote horrible things about her on the social networks.

We say "Everything is alright" because it is what we need to tell ourselves to take away some of our own heartache or at least tell us how on earth we can heal theirs. So we say "it's nothing" or "don't make a big deal out of it" or "let's look at the glass half full."

But something *did* happen, something is always happening. Not everything is okay. And when you say nothing happened, you're blocking the channel of trust between the child and life. I'm not encouraging you to cry with them, because that would be no help at all to them. But, to begin with, we can acknowledge the fact that something happened. Without panicking, without thinking of ourselves or worrying for them terribly, just by looking at the scrape on the knee or on their heart.

Listening Without Giving Advice

"When I told Mom about the girls who wouldn't play with me at school today, she immediately said, 'Tell them it's their loss and go play with someone else.'"

"When I told Daddy that David pushed me at school today and I fell, he asked, 'Well? Did you push him back?'"

"When I told Mom I don't know how I can go to school because I messed up and didn't prepare the paper that was due today, she said, 'Maybe that will finally teach you to take responsibility for your schoolwork.'"

Let's start at the end. We have a lot of educational messages, lots of ideas that we really want our children to internalize. But when an opportunity to listen comes our way, when the child chooses to share something that didn't work out well—a failure, a frustration, something that happened at kindergarten—the last thing he needs is our educational messages.

If I called a friend to tell her about a fight I had with my husband that morning and she lectured me on the importance of marriage and restraint and explained exactly what I should have done, I would probably end the conversation feeling violated. Why? Because I didn't feel that she had really listened to me, understood me, acknowledged my distress. We often see a child who, just one minute after telling us what happened, is ready to move on and has no desire or ability to listen to what we have to say. Once the story is out, the very fact that it has been shared with us makes them feel relief. There's no need to go on and on about it.

When we give a child advice in the early years, we're giving him a solution to the problem. Meaning, the problem has one solution, and not only is there only that one solution, it's in our hands and not necessarily in his. For example, we tell them: "If someone hits you—hit back!" But when a parent sends a child who is incapable of hitting back out into life—because he's just not that type of child—a new problem arises. Now, in addition to the distress of being hit or pushed, this child has to deal with a new problem—the realization that he is incapable of doing what his parent expects from him.

If you really feel an urge to give advice, make sure to first ask your child what she thinks can be done. You'll be surprised, but once they're out of the situation, children often have excellent ideas, and most importantly the kind of ideas that suit them. Also, if you decide to offer advice, ask your child first if she wants your advice, then tell her that there are many options, and try mentioning a few more.

Listening Without Overempathizing

"When I told Mom I was sad and lonely during the class trip, her eyes filled with tears. They didn't roll down, but just filled her eyes. She held them back. I broke her heart."

The story they tell when we're listening is their story. It isn't you who was alone on the class trip; it isn't you who was teased and called names. It's their story—specific, small, complicated, even difficult—but their own. Just like your parents are not you. You are really burdening them every time you overempathize with them, and it may even cause them to avoid sharing. When you feel sorry for them, they may learn to feel sorry for themselves. And when you're anxious and overprotective, they may conclude that the world is too dangerous for them. So what should you do? Try to imagine that it's the neighbor's son telling you the story—a really sweet boy whom you care about—and then listen. Just listen. Without getting overinvolved.

Listening Attentively

If children of all ages could fully express what they are feeling, they might say this:

> When I tell you something, sometimes all I need is for you to be there. Stop racing through the day, leave whatever it is you're doing at that moment, and just listen. When you listen to me correctly, when you really understand me and manage to see, smell, and feel what I experienced—without criticism or judgment, without words of wisdom, just by asking questions and helping me figure out what really happened to me there, how I felt—then I feel for a moment that we're close. I feel I can understand myself. Through your attentiveness I can set my head straight, work through the mess, and most of all I appreciate your giving me the feeling that I matter, I'm valuable, that you can count on me. That I can count on myself. So if you thought that when you just listen you're passive, think again. It's the toughest job you'll have, but I need it to grow, learn from life, count on myself, and listen to myself. And if you do it well enough, it won't be long before I'll be able to listen to you too.

Sometimes we think our children are too young, don't know enough, that they're wrong or simply not using common sense. The smallest day-to-day conversations, those that go back and forth between us during our daily routines, are gift conversations. There, of all places, they learn so much about us, about themselves, and about life.

When a child comes to tell us he got hurt and shows us a scrape or a red patch on the skin, we're not supposed to take away the pain; we're not supposed to teach him what to do so it won't happen again; we're not supposed to give him a sense of proportion. We are only supposed to be moved by the fact that he has chosen to come and tell us he got hurt and ask him with quiet concern, "How did it happen?" Children love telling us how things happened, it soothes them. They retrace the event and feel as if we were there with them at that surprising and insulting moment in which they got hurt.

While they explain how it happened, I like to ask little questions: "Does it hurt more or burn more?" "Just a second, so the drawer was open and you were running and couldn't see it was open so you just banged into it?" "Where exactly, on your forehead?" Going into such detail could sometimes seem pointless (after all, I understood exactly what happened, it definitely wasn't the first time, and would he finally learn to shut the darn drawer!), but it allows them to breathe for a second, remove themselves from the situation they're in, and look at themselves and what happened from an outer perspective. It lets them feel there's someone who sees and understands them, helps them to understand themselves and gain proportion, and makes them feel relief. By the way, this is the point where, if it doesn't really hurt, they will just move on, sometimes without even answering you, and it doesn't mean they don't respect you but that you did well, that you allowed them to get over it.

From the moment they can talk or communicate, they know what can help them, so just before you jump up with your solution ("Come, I'll give you a hug!" "Let's hit the naughty drawer back!" "Let's go have some chocolate"), ask them if there's anything that might help. And after they've gotten over it and are playing again, whisper in their ear and tell them how brave they are—how they managed to tell you exactly what happened, knew just what they needed, got over the pain or the surprise or the insult.

Drawers aren't the only things that hurt us. We get hurt by friends, teachers, siblings, and even life itself. There's no difference between the pain she gets from banging into the drawer and the pain he feels when he scores low on a test or the pain she feels when she tries to make plans with friends and nobody replies or the distress of a sixteen-year-old who tells you with tears in his eyes that he just can't take another year of school. You don't need to be his strength or shed light on everything he is supposed to be happy about or thankful for. You don't have to talk about the fact that he doesn't feel up to another year at school because last year he messed up and maybe he should do things differently this year. All you need to do is ask the right questions, those that will make him take a little trip into himself. Just stop for a moment and tell him that it's really tough, that you understand; ask if there's anything he could do differently, if there's anything you could do to help him. Just understand him, listen to him, and remember that teaching him to listen is what will make him a better friend, a better partner, and a better person.

six

Make Some Room for Dad

TEN YEARS AGO, IT WAS MOSTLY MOTHERS WHO CAME for parental counseling. One evolutionary stage later, the men began dragging themselves in after their wives, holding back yawns, keeping ongoing eye contact with their smartphones, and, at best, nodding along. But for a few years now the scent of the New Dad is in the air. Bit by bit, the new and upgraded male model is emerging: a father who is no longer content with his biological contribution alone, one who takes his relationship with his offspring seriously and passionately.

Once upon a time, this dad was "Father." Father would not enter the kitchen unless food was being served to him, would never dare ask for directions because he was obviously born with supreme navigational abilities, and when the children misbehaved, the standard-issue phrase was "Just wait till Father comes home." Had we told this Father that within a few decades he would become "Daddy," who goes to childbirth classes, cuts the umbilical cord, changes diapers, waits outside ballet class, and chops up a salad for supper—it's safe to assume he would have preferred to chop himself up.

Make no mistake, Daddy also wants his children to look up to him, obey him, meet his masculine expectations, get ahead, hit back, never give up, achieve, and conquer—and preferably with as little whining and talk of emotions as possible. But—and this is a big *but*—this new Daddy is ready and willing to take advice. He's willing to understand and tackle the complex relationship between him and his children, and most of all, he wants to be present, to take part in their education, the dilemmas, and even the day-to-day difficulties that were once strictly Mother territory.

I'm the first to congratulate the new dads and curiously await the next stage. However, and you can call me old-fashioned, I'm not taken aback when the old Father pops up: the one who raises his voice once in a while (i.e., yells loudly at the kids), doesn't give in (i.e., insists on the silliest things), and draws the line a little too rigidly ("The child is almost blue in the face from crying. Would you go to her?"), especially when there's an empathetic motherly model at his side. Our children need parents who make decisions together and jointly formulate rules and boundaries, but they also need to see variation, diversity, different ways of coping, and most of all to see how you can respect another person's different way of doing things. Let's remind ourselves of three advantages the male model has.

Mission-Driven

It might be their lacking a sense of fashion or their failure to notice details—but to Daddy, usually, clothes are just clothes. When a father dresses a child, he doesn't care what the other parents or the kindergarten teacher will think. He doesn't try to delicately steer the child toward the shirt he likes best and isn't disappointed when the child's shirt and pants don't match. As far as he is concerned, you have to get dressed because you can't walk around with nothing on, and if it were up to him there wouldn't be fifty options in the closet but only seven—one for each day of the week.

With Daddy, the atmosphere around getting dressed is mission-driven and decisive, and both parties—parent and child—are on the same side of the court. On the other hand, when we approach a situation with a desire to govern the pace, what the child will wear, and the atmosphere, too—the title is "control" and we find ourselves on the other side of the court, opposite our child, just like in a tennis match: they serve, we strike back; they hit harder, we somehow manage to lob it back, but they don't give in, and so the match continues, and at the end we either lose or come out exhausted. It wouldn't hurt to give up a little control. But this can only work if we really don't care about what they wear, what they look like, and how embarrassing it will be (to us).

"Dressing children" is a label we can easily replace with any other daily task: getting out of the house, getting into the bath, getting medical care, or saying goodbye in the morning. They all share the basic idea that the parent does not get emotionally overinvolved. We're both here to get the job done, even if it isn't fun, and I'm not against you, I'm just helping you to get it done.

Filtering

Men have the amazing capacity to sit in one space with their child while managing to get something else done—read a book, talk on the phone, write an email, clip their nails, replace batteries—

through their ability to filter out unnecessary requests, whining, fights, calls for help, and other background noises.

The model of a parent who has a life fosters children who know the world does not necessarily revolve around them. The parent is not attentive twenty-four hours a day to every whim, activity, or demand for action. Daddy is able to set his boundaries and from that moment on be busy with something that is only about him. And thus, over time, the children learn to occupy themselves, solve problems, fight without a parent getting involved, and sometimes polish off a packet of cookies without anyone noticing.

Let them see you focus on something that isn't them: talking to your friend, really enjoying eating something that is more than their leftovers, having trouble with something and trying to solve it, going into the bathroom and closing the door. When they become accustomed to seeing you as a human being, they will find their own problems easier to handle. They will learn to be considerate of others, deal with boredom (without you having to entertain them), and manage frustration more easily. And the things that will stick in their memories are all the times you *did* make yourself available to them (without accumulated resentment, because you've already taken some time for yourself) and played with them, went for ice cream, or made up a story together. And that's the best part.

Courage

My father was in the army. He was tall and strong, he had a ladder and tools and could fix anything. My father never cried, and when he was angry it was really scary, so we tried very hard not to make him angry. He never asked if I was offended or why I was mad or if something was difficult for me. When his tone became clipped, I tried my best to hurry up, and once a week, on Saturday mornings, after ten o'clock, I was allowed to slip into his bed, put my head under his arm, and have a cuddle.

He called me "Courage," and not because I was brave. Every time I heard "Courage, come on! Don't give up," I knew there was no option of giving up. Even if I had just fallen off my bike and my knee hurt, even if I had swallowed some water in the pool, even if I made five mistakes in a row in math—I was Courage, and Courage takes a deep breath, sucks it up, and pushes on. Because what defines courage is not the lack of fear or despair but the ability to feel the fear and despair and stick with it anyway.

When fathers throw their child high up in the air, for a few moments when that little body is in midair, her expression changes a little: she's scared—and then Daddy's hands catch her again.

I can't stand the sight of a child in midair; it makes my stomach turn. And when they swallow water when learning to swim or dive, all I want to do is pull them out of the swimming pool, wrap them up in a big towel, and kiss their chlorine-dripping body. To me, it's perfectly all right if they can't ride a bike without training wheels, and I can relate when they want to come home in the middle of a class trip because they're homesick and can already feel it in their throat and are about to cry in front of all of their friends. But then I remember—they need to know what courage feels like, they need someone who won't feel sorry for them so they can stop feeling sorry for themselves. They need to be thrown in the air for a few milliseconds of fear, and then have someone catch them again.

seven

Sharing One Bed

FOR THIRTY NIGHTS WE SLEPT SIDE BY SIDE, MY FATHER and I, just after I was born. My mom was sick, too exhausted to be there for me at night, so he and I slept in another room. I, in the crib, and he, jumping up to heat a bottle every time I whimpered, cradling me in his arms, and offering me the bottle at just the right temperature. Close up, his manly white undershirt, the hairs on his chest blending with the warmth of his body. His soothing heartbeats and comfort became an emotional memory of love and security.

At the age of three, four, or five, I remember my feet on the cold floor, taking me in the middle of the night to their bed after a bad dream, scary thought, or just a noise. I would crawl in the middle, between him and her, and immediately calm down, as if given a soothing medicine. It was always with my back to her and my face, nose, and cheek to him. The body remembered. To this day, when it feels like the skies are coming down on me, on really black days, I sometimes get the feeling that if only he in his white undershirt hugged me, everything would be okay.

From zero to nine months, we are raising little cubs. Our cubs, the ones who were placed on us the second after they were born, soothing themselves with the touch of our skin, the sound of our heartbeat, these are the same little cubs we take home to a fashionable, pulseless bed with rails. When they wake up at night, we go to them, feed them, hug them, and put them back down again, hoping that they will get used to the feeling of the mattress instead of their mother's touch, the scent of the clean sheets instead of the familiar, precious scent of our body. Take a look at nature for a moment, that thing we used to be a part of before we moved into houses and started drinking cappuccinos. No animal in nature places her young cubs in a distant place, expecting them to go to sleep by themselves while she goes to sleep elsewhere.

At the beginning of a cub's life, their sense of well-being in the world depends exclusively on a figure that will guard them and protect them from danger. Nothing can compete with the feeling of a protective mother nearby, her familiar breaths or the scent of her body. Think of them as tourists in a country where they don't understand the language, not even the noises or the lights; even the way their own body feels can scare them. The only thing they have at their disposal is the tour guide assigned to them at the airport, the parents who guard them from evil, whose scent they recognize, and whose caresses they humbly accept and interpret as love and security.

We, the tour guides, are suddenly bound to our tiny tourist, turning into physical and emotional service providers working 24/7. There is no parent who hasn't experienced the exhausting intensiveness of rearing babies and catering to their every need. Lack of sleep is one of the most common parental difficulties in the beginning, and the feeling of exhaustion is truly unnerving and can make even the most Dalai Lama of parents lose their equilibrium. Parents who don't get enough sleep are prone to depression and anxiety, their frustration threshold is especially low, and their ability to function is identical to that of an intoxicated person who would never pass any Breathalyzer test.

Some babies find it easy enough to fall asleep, and when they wake up in the middle of the night, they manage to go back to sleep by themselves, without requiring any real comforting. They don't wake up crying hysterically, and they indicate what their needs are clearly and allow us to rest in between. But what about all the cubs that have a hard time and find that the soft touch of the sweet star-patterned pajamas we lovingly dressed them in after the bath simply isn't soft enough for them? What about those who don't fall asleep easily, don't sleep without interruptions, the ones we find ourselves feeding seven times a night? What woke these babies up in the first place was not hunger but a sense of lack, discomfort, a new tooth coming out, something uncomfortable in their diaper, their body jolting involuntarily. All these things have only one remedy in nature: touch.

When we try things with a baby, we enter an ongoing dialogue. He cries, and immediately we see what can make him feel better: sometimes it's the breast or the bottle; sometimes it's a hug or stroking the back of his neck; sometimes a pacifier and kiss are enough; and sometimes we have to resort to the rocking wave motions they remember from their time in the womb. And there are a lot of babies that we can just take into bed with us and, after we take off our shirts and lay them beside us or on top of us (assuming you're not the kind of people who move around a lot in your sleep or won't wake up from anything), there will be no doubt that that was all they needed.

With such "touch babies," we encounter the slippery slope, which starts with bringing them into our bed and ends with a whole night of surprisingly sweet, uninterrupted sleep. This sleep will turn into a habit that allows both sides to get a bit of rest: us, from the extremely hard job of being parents, and them, from the extremely hard job of being helpless little creatures. Because there, between the doctors' warnings and the experts' cautions, lies nature: a little cub and a parent watching over her.

You can change habits. People change their habits when they discover that the price they are paying is higher than the gain. Sleep consultancy, weaning consultancy, and many other wonderful forms of guidance that are sensitive to the child's and parents' needs will always be available. So you can relax when people warn you "You don't want a seven-year-old sleeping in your bed" or "it will be very hard on him on school trips," and you can remember that it's much easier to teach children to sleep alone when they understand language, when you can explain the meaning of nighttime, prepare them, listen to their fears, understand what could help them, cheer them with every improvement, and celebrate the first night in a separate room and a separate bed. Yes, even if it's when she turns two and a half. The more separate, independent, and able she becomes, the easier it will be for her to count on herself to survive, to shut her eyes and know that she's not really in danger, because she has herself. Separation anxiety is not an anxiety our cubs should encounter in the first few months of their lives.

I'm not going into parenting and lifestyle considerations here. Obviously, I, too, like you, would be happy with a child who slept through the night from month one on, "knock on wood, we didn't have to do anything to make it happen." But what can you do? Each child is born with their own qualities and sensibilities, an individual regulation system, a particular rhythm, difficulties, fears, thoughts, and a personality of their very own. Are the good parents the ones whose children sit quietly in the stroller, sleep through the night, and fall asleep the moment you start the car's engine? The answer: not at all.

In the space between the baby bed with the rails in the other room and a child who sleeps with his parents until he turns seven lie a few more points worth inspecting, worth checking out without guilt, without listening to the neighbor who says, "We went through four nights of hell and screaming, but she has been sleeping through the night ever since." But how do we investigate these other options? With attentiveness to your baby, a deep understanding that a baby's night should be free of anxiety, that touch can even heal disease and pain, that parenting a baby is a tough business, and that a baby should not be disciplined. Believe me, you'll never come across an adolescent who crawls into his parents' bed at night, and adolescence comes so quickly that it's worth just taking a deep breath now and being patient.

Our babies are our cubs during the night, too, so maybe we should listen to them when they whimper and commit ourselves without words to becoming a complete and safe world for them.

eight

Life's Goodbyes

WHEN I PARTED WITH MY MOTHER, I WAS ALREADY A grown-up. I had two children, a husband, a life of my own. The parting took place in stages, as is the case with severe illnesses: it prepares us, the hover of death lingering in the air for years, dispersing a scent of longing even while everyone is still around.

On the way home from the funeral, our last moment of togetherness, mother and daughter, I tried as hard as I could to remember the days she'd pick me up from kindergarten, from school, from the bus stop. I tried, but couldn't. Through the car window, I looked at the power lines passing by as if I had become again that little girl in the backseat, not sure where we were going, not sure when we would get there, just counting the utility poles as we drove.

Later it became clear to me that my mother and I would meet again but that the encounter would only take place inside me. Just as I had spent nine months inside her, now I would have to find her inside me, but this time there wouldn't be life at the end of the journey, just longing. A mother inside a daughter instead of a daughter inside a mother.

Our children's lives are woven through with thousands of little goodbyes. Good goodbyes, empowering goodbyes, but hard ones. There is a reason why they say that every goodbye is to die a little. Parting with a toy snatched by another child; saying goodbye in the morning to go to kindergarten; saying goodnight when it's time to sleep; saying goodbye to a friend when Mom says it's time to go; saying goodbye to Dad when the day with him is over according to the custody schedule; parting with the child I was to my parents before my sister was born; losing a tooth. "Mom, look how sad the tree is," my eldest son said to me when he noticed autumn for the first time in his life. "His leaves are leaving him. I wonder if he knows that soon he'll have new ones."

But what do we say to our children about these goodbyes? We say things like "stop crying" or "promise me that today you'll say goodbye nicely" or "it makes me really sad when you cry." And even when we don't say these things, we communicate our disappointment, our impatience toward their difficulty. So let's make a little more sense of it:

1. They can't and shouldn't stop crying. That's what you do when you say goodbye.
2. They can't and shouldn't promise that today they'll say goodbye nicely. Every day they hope and pray that they'll manage to live up to that expectation and keep their promise, but when they don't manage, when it doesn't work out, it feels as if they have broken a promise, making it hurt even more.

3. When you tell them it makes you sad, they have to deal
   not only with their own sadness but with the sadness they
   have caused you too. Quite a burden for a three-year-old,
   isn't it?

The idea we should pass on to our children is this: "Parting
is sad, for us parents, too. You're allowed to cry. We trust you
to get over it, and we know you'll have a nice time when the
sadness blows over. At lunch or in the afternoon, we'll see each
other again." It's not always pleasant, it sometimes makes your
heart ache, but it's not something the parent is doing "against" the
child. It's just part of life.

Many children live with the wrong and burdening assumption that if they only cry hard enough, beg, keep us busy, or resist, they will manage to avoid the goodbye. We are the ones who
taught them this erroneous lesson, because when they had a hard
time in the morning and cried, we told them we had to go, but
then they cried a little harder and we said, "Okay, we'll make one
drawing together and then I'll go." But when it was really time
to leave and they cried harder still and even begged, we didn't
stay; we broke the contract. And at night, when we said, "Night,
night, everyone's gone to sleep now," they asked for water just
one more time and we brought it to them, and then they cried
and said they were scared and we came back to the room for five
more minutes, and after that they were really crying and said
they had one more really important thing to tell us or that their
tummy hurt or that they had to pee or that they heard a strange
noise, and by then we were angry and said, "Stop it! Enough already! You're driving me crazy!"

A child who's busy showing how hard the separation is for him isn't free to overcome it. He isn't available to remember that it's a separation in life and that in the morning the sun will rise and we'll meet again. When I set a boundary, I don't expect the child to be happy or pleased. I explain it to him and prepare him in advance and won't ask him to stop crying, because every time I say goodbye I also cry a little inside. I make a commitment to see him, to understand that he's sad, and to encourage him every time he overcomes it, and this is the way I can teach him to become stronger and survive life's little and big goodbyes.

The feeling that might form in children is that to us everything is simple, everything is resolved, and, as a result, when they don't manage to cope with the hardships involved in goodbyes, they can be overwhelmed by a strong feeling of loneliness. Talk to them not while they're having the difficulty but before or after—and tell them that it's also hard on you, that you also think about them suddenly in the middle of the day and miss them. Ask them for advice: "Maybe I should take a picture of you with me? Maybe you can kiss me on the elbow and then I'll look at the elbow and think of you? Maybe I'll say to myself, 'We'll see each other soon'? And then maybe on the way to work I'll skip a little because skipping takes the sadness away?" Suggest that they can also use all the ideas you've come up with if they feel like it. This makes them feel important, because you asked them for advice, and normal, because they will realize they're not the only one who gets sad.

When you're parting for a few days, agree beforehand to have one phone call a day. Tell them it will be hard for you to call more than that because you'll miss them so much (the idea is actually to spare them the hardship of having you call every two minutes to check in), and consult them about the best time for the phone call (a call too late in the evening when they are tired could be unpleasant). Preparing a countdown calendar can help younger children get a better sense of time, and you can also suggest that they draw a picture every time they miss you, thereby channeling the sadness into an active rather than a passive experience. And of course, don't forget to bring home a symbolic present worth waiting for.

There's a reason why kids ask to take a toy airplane with them to kindergarten or to hear the same story over and over again. Everything they take with them, even when it's buried deep in their bag or their pocket, gives them the feeling that they've taken a part of home with them, as if there's suddenly a bridge connecting them to Dad and Mom: it's no longer "kindergarten that *isn't* home," it's kindergarten that has a piece of home in it. And this piece gives them strength, they can hold on to it.

As they grow up and we do our parental job properly, training them in separations both small and large, they will realize that even when they are apart from us, even if it hurts, we stay there with them, inside them. And when we are there inside them, they have themselves with us. So don't get confused when they cry, don't try to take away their sadness, don't hurry to buy them a hamster that looks just like the one that died or a new toy to replace the one that broke.

My mother was a small woman, short, so thin. When I saw her wrapped in the funeral sheet, I wondered how such a great woman could be so small. She knew how to be moved by everything: people, words, music, memories. Her nose turned red every time she cried, and she cried plenty, because of a song she heard on the radio or a friend's gesture; her tear ducts worked very well. She had beautiful hands, and when we would sing holiday songs together, she would always tap her nails to the rhythm. She liked having real conversations with her friends, and once a day she would light a cigarette in the living room, open a window, and ask me to sit down beside her and tell her all about the interesting things that had happened to me that day.

My third daughter has her hands, my second son took her red nose, and I inherited the ability to be moved like her, by people, a good chat, songs on the radio. And there's nothing I love more than sitting with a child and hearing stories about the interesting things that happened to them that day. The reason I couldn't remember my goodbyes from her was probably because she did them so well, and the last goodbye was the hardest of all.

nine

Growing Through Anger

A T 6:15 A.M., SHE AND I ARE IN THE CAR. I'M FORTY-four. She turned ten in April. The large parking lot is packed with children and parents, buses, rucksacks, and sleeping bags. She had deliberated whether to go on the three-day camping trip, asking if it would be okay if she went away on my birthday. I had said I'd be happy to know on my birthday that she was happy, and immediately opened my GPS to check how long it would take to drive to the place where they were camping. After all, it was obvious that she would call us to pick her up after the sun set the first day out; there was no chance she would manage three whole days away from home.

When we got out of the car, I helped her with her bag. She detected the cool group straightaway and walked a little faster. I walked with her until her body signaled it was time to say good-bye. I hugged her. She didn't hug me back. I whispered in her ear that I loved her so much and walked back to the car, not before looking back again to catch her gaze. She had already joined the group. I could barely see the way back to the car through the tears that flooded my eyes. When I shut the door behind me, I was already wailing. Something about the ten-year-old, plus the Scout's uniform, plus the buses caught me off guard. I didn't expect to lose it like that.

How was it possible that just a moment ago I was the one leaving her for work, a meeting, errands, and she was the one crying, getting angry, stomping her feet? She would shout "Mooommmy!" and I would set the boundaries. I was the clear one, the one leaving, and she was the dependent one, the one in tears. And now, through the turning doors of life, she was so clear, so separate, going off to do her own thing while I was left behind, stomping my feet and in tears, even a little angry about the intolerable ease with which she said goodbye.

Separation is a complex process that starts at birth, the first separation between a mother and child, and ends with the parents going and the child remaining. Our end goal is to help our kids lead a wonderful and full life without us, and still carry our voices within them. We cry in the car when they go to kindergarten for the first time, start school, go off to camp, enlist in the army, go out in the evening, get married, travel abroad. They miss us and have a good time.

The beginning is pretty simple—we take care of their every need and they become attached to us. An exhausting but very clear process. When they turn two, more or less, the winds of change start blowing. Unlike the initial contract, where the child is a consumer and the parent a supplier, now sometimes the child needs something and the parent can't provide. The new reality creates friction. And here, in this hard place, the child grows.

When we set limits and the toddler tests them, the initial separation becomes explicit. We define our boundaries, marking the place where we end, and they begin to understand where they begin. So now he wants an ice cream and we say he can't have one? The child turns to his separate operating system and gets angry, disappointed, or frustrated. The external operating system quickly responds, and he protests: crying, throwing himself on the floor, hitting, telling you that you're horrid. This is where we make our common mistakes: we get angry in response, we ask him to calm down right now, we send him to his room, or we give in and get him that ice cream. Exhausted and helpless, we simply can't understand how our sweet little bundle—who was laughing and playing just ten minutes ago, doing as he was told or expressing his protest in a very symbolic way at most before moving on—transformed into this disgruntled, shrieking little mass.

Understand this: protest, anger, and tantrums are all developmental achievements. Here's your child, standing opposite you, encountering a boundary you set and finding it objectionable, because she is separate and has separate wants, so everything you do at that point to take away the experience only spoils the growth. She is learning a new skill right now, just like learning how to walk or dress herself, and our hope is that at the end of this process, when she encounters frustration she'll know how to handle it, how to overcome the sense of helplessness, reach calculated decisions, stay optimistic, and, most of all, not blame others for the unwanted reality or take it personally. But this doesn't happen in a day.

Understand Their Frustration

When they cry, are unhappy, argue, whine, or start kicking and shouting—it's not because they woke up that morning with an intent to wreck your day. There is a concrete reason for their frustration—it's not you, it's the boundary. It's not that they won't accept your parental authority, it's just that they are facing frustration, and you, who removed every obstacle until now, are not providing that service any longer. Tell your child, "I understand that you are angry/disappointed/sad/jealous," keeping it short. It is important to name the specific emotion in each situation so that they understand what they are feeling right now and know how to verbalize it at the next stage instead of screaming. Don't say these words in the patronizing tone a teacher might use ("I understand that you're angry, but there's nothing we can do about it").

Instead, give them the feeling that you really understand them; pass on the "but" and just say, "Wow, you're really, really angry right now. It's annoying that it isn't possible, isn't it?" and mean it.

Say Yes

When you say what's not allowed, add a logical explanation and mention what *is* allowed. "I'm not getting you an ice cream right now, but you can have some watermelon." They don't have to agree to what you're suggesting, but making the suggestion is more respectful of them. This is where we plant the seed for the optimistic child's personality, the child who knows that even when we are in the most difficult and complex of situations, and everything around seems to be "no," there's always a choice, you can always find a "yes" somewhere. And when they calm down a little and their level of anxiety decreases, they'll choose between one of the positive options set before them.

Fuss Over Them When They Get Over It, Not When They're Crying

You can offer a hug, a kiss, or any other form of comfort—they can choose which. And when they have calmed down and come to you for that hug or that yes option you offered, don't forget to roll out the red carpet. Tell them that the fact that they are overcoming the trouble, showing flexibility, and turning a new page isn't being taken for granted. They need to hear what the new ability they just managed to adopt actually is called, to know that it means they are growing and getting stronger. If they calm down and stop shouting, be impressed and say that this is called "being a child who knows how to calm herself." If they choose another way of backing down and, after forty minutes of crying, yelling, and protesting, they are content and happy with what they get, say, "It's amazing to see you turn a new page—I've got a child who knows how to be content, even if she doesn't get the ice cream she wanted."

This is actually what builds the foundation for the most important parental duty of all: being impressed, encouraging, and supportive every time our children improve, overcome, restrain themselves, cooperate, make the right choice, express contentedness, create a new reality. On the other hand, when they cry, shout, or throw themselves on the floor, we allow it and understand their frustration and anger, but we won't become emotionally involved, we won't get angry, punish, or, alternatively, pull bunnies and sweets out of our hats—because this is their thing. Their journey is becoming a separate one, and we can't get confused about that. We have to remember that when they get angry, it's not *against* us but *for* themselves.

When we get angry in response, punish them, or tell them it makes us very sad to see them react like that, we contaminate their learning space. We're not allowing them their separateness and end up making the whole thing about our relationship. These little lessons start at the age of two with tantrums and continue through the age of three, when they walk into preschool by themselves; the age of five, when they stay at a birthday party without us; the age of seven, when they don't do their homework and the teacher makes a note of it; and the age of ten, when they go on a camping trip, overcome plenty of challenges, and, to your surprise, stay the whole three days.

— *ten* —

How to Talk to Them

I KNEW THAT LOOK SO WELL, WHEN SHE GOT DISAP-
pointed, when she took me too seriously, when she got personally offended by the adolescent that I was. The look on my
mother's face would take the whole conflict between us and
make it null and void. The moment I stepped over the limit, there
was nothing but that expression there: horrified, angry, rejecting
me. Insulted.

That look signaled that now it was about her, not about the
argument we had, not about my needs, not even about what I was
feeling. Now I would have to crawl over and try to compensate
her for the terrible word that came out of my mouth while I was
angry, just so that she could love me again. And even when I managed, with gestures and begging, to obtain her forgiveness, there
was the scar that her expression left in us, both of us. A scar that
wounded the relationship.

One of the most unrewarding parts of being a parent is the
job of being a toxin filter, a sponge that takes in all the muck.
And that's true at any age, because even at thirty-five a woman
will, in her mother's presence, release toxins that are aimed at

her ears only. It might be frustration, unresolved accounts, a hard day, or some other emotional waste that you could handle any other day bravely and confidently; but just put your mother in front of you and the little girl oozes out.

In the task of parenting, the consequential decision is what kind of a sponge we choose to be, finding the right balance, which is oh-so-hard to pinpoint, between soft and hard. How do we manage to allow our children to feel comfortable enough, on the one hand, to release their frustrations on us and, on the other hand, stand tall and not get confused by the rancid waste that has just been poured all over us? When he's just four, he'll call me "meanie" when I don't allow him to take another chocolate pudding; at seven, she'll say "I hate you" when I don't let her have a friend sleep over on a weekday; at thirteen, he'll say the most awful things when we don't let him ride his bicycle without a helmet; and at seventeen, she'll scream at me that I don't understand anything and that she's sorry I'm her mother because I won't let her go on a sleepover rave packed with booze and boys. How are we supposed to take in all that toxicity without collapsing? How do we allow the negative emotions to come out while remembering that they are not against us?

This is truly one of the most challenging tasks we have as parents, because it requires us to put ourselves and our sensitivities to the side and realize that when we make it about us, we're not educating. It's true, even the best sponge needs a bucket nearby where it can empty itself once in a while, but we don't have the privilege of getting insulted by our children. We are not in a couple relationship with them, we are not their friends, and even though the value of equality is at the very base of the family unit, we are not their equals. We are on duty. We are the parents and they are the children.

When children encounter an unwanted reality, their anxiety level increases. They come face-to-face with the unfortunate fact that the world was not created to cater to their immediate wants; they feel lonely and angry and, going against every rule of politeness, words of anger come out of their mouths. They are aimed at us, the parents, but their whole point is to vent an immense feeling of frustration. And we are supposed to contain this frustration and take it, not because we are our children's punching bag, but because our primary task is to teach them, while they are confronted with the rules, that it's nothing personal, it's just the way it is—because it's dangerous or unhealthy or goes against our values.

It's not between us and them. On the contrary: the main point in being the sponge is to join them in the frustration, take in the hardship without altering the boundary to help decrease the level of anxiety and help them get over it.

But instead, we, who are supposed to teach them that it's nothing personal, often stop everything when we hear the unpleasant and insulting words "You're a doo-doo head!" and ask, "What did you just say?! What did you call me?" Dad shouts from the living room, "That's no way to talk to your mother!" Mom adds, "Go to your room right now and think long and hard about the words that just came out of your mouth!" or she uses the heavyweights: "It really hurts me when you use words like that. You've made me angry and sad. How would you feel if I told you that I hated you?" Reacting this way to the insult turns the whole thing into a personal drama. This teaches the child that it *is* personal. That when an unwanted reality comes along you're on your own, because when you get angry and take it out on me, I turn the whole boundaries thing into an issue between you and me. I have taught you to get angry about boundaries and to not accept them, to take it personally instead of searching for the places inside you that could help you cope and overcome. And especially, I have taught you that when you're angry and take your frustration out on me, my love and acceptance are suddenly conditional and our relationship is tentative.

On the other hand, when I turn to a child who just called me an idiot and say, "I understand that it's making you very angry that you can't have another chocolate pudding," her anxiety level decreases. Unlike what she just did, I don't fuel the personal issue, but say, "I'm with you, I understand you, it's so annoying." I don't expect her to calm down, I don't expect her to say, "Okay, Mom, I really have had enough sweet things today." But when I do not respond to the toxins she released on me but to the emotional reason that prompted them, she can encounter the frustration without feeling alone.

A parent's honor does not lie in the words a three-year-old uses in the heat of a tantrum—it arises from our ability to set the boundary and to not get confused into thinking that when our child isn't happy about our boundary he's being disrespectful toward us; it stems from our ability to understand that focusing on the insulting words that just came out of her mouth and getting ourselves mixed up in the equation prevent her from coming face-to-face with reality and coping with it. When we avoid focusing on the words themselves or on our sense of honor and instead respond to the upset child with "I understand that you're angry/disappointed/sad/jealous/upset/annoyed because we can't do what you wanted," gradually the child realizes what she actually felt and that those are the right words to describe the experience she just had. In our ability to put our idea of respect aside and see her for a moment, that's where true parental dignity lies.

I remember the first time he said "I hate you." He was three and a half, we were coming back from kindergarten, and I was preoccupied. We walked hand in hand down the path, he spoke fast and walked slowly, and I was so hot. When he asked to stop at the corner shop, I put my hand in my bag to take out my purse, hoping that I would find some coins there that would buy me a few minutes of him chewing and me remembering who I was again, listing all the things I had to get done that afternoon. But my purse wasn't there; I had forgotten it.

I tried to explain that there was no purse because Mommy's a bit confused. If I could have, I would have explained that there was no purse because I was up all night with his baby sister or maybe there was no purse because I was worried about his older brother after having a talk with the kindergarten teacher, who said that he was having a really hard time lately. Maybe I'd add that I sat in the car before going into the kindergarten, angry at myself for not having the energy to go in, for needing a few more minutes of peace and quiet in the air-conditioned car. Or maybe I'd just tell him that the holidays were coming up, and I really missed my mother over the holidays. And the purse was forgotten at home.

He reacted like he never had before. When he was younger, the tears always came rolling very fast, but since his little blonde sister was born he was mostly angry and almost never cried. He looked at me with bright eyes, blinking fast as if instructing the blue bowls not to shed any tears, and screamed, "Mom, I hate you!" I think he was also taken aback, because it was the first time he had hated me out loud.

I bent over so I could look straight into his eyes and told him that it really was very annoying that I had forgotten my purse and that I understood that he wanted to get something in the corner shop. I suggested that we sit on the sidewalk and just feel angry together about the purse and all the things we could have bought with the coins in it. We sat there together, an exhausted mother and a disappointed child. He wasn't angry anymore, and the tears came. And there, on that sidewalk, when he and I encountered life together, there was a lot of dignity.

eleven

Let Boys Cry

YUVAL DOESN'T CRY. EVEN WHEN WE WATCH FILMS that make me finish a whole box of tissues, his eyes don't become even slightly moist. I married a real man, and real men don't cry. It's actually hard for me to imagine, for example, a man crying because his boss offended him or because his wife wasn't paying enough attention to him lately.

When one of the girls bursts into tears, Yuval is the first to hug and soften toward her. On the other hand, when one of the boys cries, I feel him shift with unease and worry, seeing his own weaknesses—the ones he managed to repress and bury with years of hard work. What could he do about the simple fact that young boys and girls have the exact same crying habits?

At the start of life, crying serves babies in getting what they need to survive. Their crying helps us attune ourselves to them and care for them in the way they need to be cared for. As they grow up, the reasons for crying multiply as their emotional world becomes more and more complex; this is when we usually start getting a little nervous. Think of a four-year-old boy crying because he got hit by a ball, played a game that he lost, got a vaccination that hurt, or was insulted by a friend. We tend to castrate this crying in various ways, with a disparaging look, with impatience, and with wonderful remarks like "Shake it off, little man," or "You're crying like a girl over something like that?"

We signal to them that they shouldn't cry, that it's not good to cry, and every time they feel sad or angry inside, every time the tears flood their eyes and their chin quivers, they have to hold it back. But with the pressure cooker closed, the steam still searches for a way out, and it will find a way eventually—in the form of aggression. This is something we can handle when it comes to boys, isn't it? So he throws a chair, gets into a fight in kindergarten, pushes when someone tries to take his turn on the swings, but at least he isn't crying.

It's not only the wonder of crying that we withhold from our boys but also the entirety of emotional communication that crying usually prompts: empathy, our listening, the understanding that it is allowed and worthwhile to show vulnerability when it invites a close person into dialogue. We withhold the process of learning that emotional communication is a blessed thing that will advance him; but mostly, we withhold the opportunity for him to get to know himself a little better.

Tears cloud your field of vision. This might be why animals don't cry—it would make them easy prey. But when it comes to us humans, this blurring of the external lets us see better inward, into our souls, and this might be an even smarter survival mechanism. Crying is there to let us air our emotional system, stop all our automatic functions and just be, to listen to ourselves.

So before we laugh again about how emotionally dense men are, we might take some responsibility for swapping the tears with anger and aggression too soon, for inadvertently making men less good to themselves, to their future partners, to society as a whole. And if we allow them, and ourselves in front of them, to express emotion, to cry, to understand themselves and others thanks to tears, the world just might become a better place.

Since my boys were very young, every year in their birthday cards I have wished them one more year of allowing themselves to cry. They never really got it, and Yuval also makes a face every time he hears the greeting. Today they almost never cry, but once in a while I see a touch of moistness in their eyes before the inner policeman of masculinity pulls them over and asks to see their license. And I pray with all my heart that what I wished for them all these years will meet them in private situations in life, with themselves or with their chosen ones, and that they will be able to let that policeman rest for a little while, knowing clearly that even when they cry they are still real men. Maybe even especially real men.

twelve

"Come On, Let's Go!"

S HE WOKE UP FROM A BAD DREAM, AND HER CRYING overcame the sound of the pouring rain. "Mommy, someone swapped you in my dream," she cried. "You were you, but angry. You looked like my mother but kept shouting at us all the time. You were so scary. A monster-mom."

I held her tight, gave her a glass of water, and thought to myself how right she was, how this nightmare had come to her for a reason. In the last few days I had been so busy, so mission-oriented, that I turned into a monster-mom. How easy it is to forget about the joy when there are so many things to get done.

We need to tidy up the house, do the laundry, go over emails, get to work. We need some peace and quiet, time with our partner, a five-minute shower. And they get in the way of completing the tasks of life. So why won't they put their shoes on already, go to sleep, get out of the car because we need to be somewhere, move on, move ahead? And we say, "Come on, will you?" "Why now?" "Stop it, that's enough!" "I said right now!" "I'm counting to three." "If you don't, I'll . . ." and without even noticing, we turn into these tall people with an angry crease between our brows who push, who get things done. People who have forgotten how to laugh or act silly for no particular reason. People who are not having fun.

We sometimes get the feeling that if we go along with them, dress them while we're singing a funny song together, or stop for a second to notice the shadow the table is casting on the wall, they will win and we will become parents without boundaries who are raising kids who don't know when enough is enough. In fact, we waste much more energy and time when we stand opposite them, focused on the clock and the tasks ahead, than we would if we were on their side against the clock. We would reach our destination at exactly the same time, but with a feeling of winning against the clock instead of winning or losing our child.

Even if I have to force my child to put her shoes on and put her in the car against her will, it feels totally different if I tell her I love her, that she's my sweetie, but we still have to get to kindergarten on time. And the moment she calms down, I won't give her a lecture about being on time or ask why every morning has to be such a nightmare but will immediately turn a new page and tell her how amazing she is—even though it didn't suit her, she still went ahead and did it, and now that she's calmed down, I've got to tell her about this dream I dreamed last night, because it was really funny. Just think how many things I taught her just now about coping with life.

It really is a matter of adjusting yourself, investing energy, and having a profound understanding of who's up against whom. The idea is to set out on the tasks of life with the goal of not only finishing supper, a shower, a story, and bedtime but also teaching them that limits or routines are not something personal against them. They gain control not by resisting us but by choosing the shirt or the story. They get to choose pleasure instead of suffering, happiness instead of frustration.

Patience is not a quality you are either born with or without—it's not like the color of your hair or eyes. It's worth remembering that although the price of impatience is paid by both sides, the higher price is paid by the children. If the role model they see before them every day is efficient, effective, frustrated, and angry, they will grow up to become people who are unable to be patient toward themselves, others, and unwanted realities.

The most painful times that test our patience are usually mornings and evenings. These are when young children face tasks of life that they have no interest in performing and that we want to complete as fast as possible. This conflict of interests dictates a situation in which we are constantly trying to move toward the next task while they do everything they can to stall. No child gets up every morning, quickly chooses his clothes, gets dressed alone, brushes his teeth, and puts on his shoes, cheerfully and in under twenty minutes. The children who get these tasks done quickly, without dilly-dallying or complaining, are the neglected children, the ones whose parent is absent or has no interest in keeping the schedule.

Mornings aren't necessarily the best time to teach children independence or to insist on high-quality performance. In the places where interests conflict, we should make it easier on ourselves, too. They can get dressed by themselves when you are going to an amusement park on the weekend and they are really dying to go. Sometimes their crying or discontentment is my morning's soundtrack, and I have to remind myself that

I'm with them, not against them, and that if we get all the annoying stops along the way—getting dressed, putting our shoes
on, and brushing our teeth—over and done fast enough, I can
promise them a tickling game or a funny dance in the kitchen.
And then, even if they do insist on having their hair redone for
the millionth time, I can explain that what's going to happen
next is that I'll choose for them if they can't choose for themselves, and we won't be able to change it again, because we
want to reach some "happy stop" together, the last stop, where
the pleasure is found.

They came to us, these kids, to teach us something, remind
us of something we used to know. We laughed a lot when we
were a couple without kids, we were fun when we were twenty,
we just stared into open space when we were seventeen, and we
imagined whole worlds when we were nine. We were in the here
and now, the pleasure of a sweet flavor, the joy of indulging in a
hug, swimming in water, riding a bike with the wind in our hair,
playing make-believe games, picking a branch off the ground and
imagining it's a magic wand. The kids came to remind us what
fun is all about, what the meaning of laughing, curiosity, and new
discoveries really is.

Knowing that the mother my children see is a happy mother,
even when she has to get annoying tasks done, helps me every day
(well, almost every day) not to go out of my mind; it helps me
remember not to be against them, not to be the grumpy woman
who has to get to work on time. Parents who find happiness in
these hard places are the ones who manage to raise children who
are happy with their lot. Our little ones will be all grown-up in
a moment. Soon we won't be combing their hair, rushing them,

putting a sandwich in their backpack. At best, we'll hear a "bye" when they leave the house. So in the meantime, let them head off from a happy house so that they manage to find happiness in themselves when things get tough, so that joy is always an option for them, one they can choose as grown-ups, just as they chose it so naturally when they were still little.

thirteen

"Go On, Say Sorry"

WHY IS IT SO DIFFICULT FOR ME TO ADMIT IT WHEN I'M
wrong? I'm lying in the bedroom, the fifth one is trying
to fall asleep, and I'm next to her. These are the moments when
thoughts concerning the day ahead usually run through my mind:
Rona—holiday ceremony at school—white shirt; Lihi—apples
and honey; Yoav—money for the literature textbook; Shira—
empty milk carton; Eyal—signed declaration of health. But
today, after the terrible fight I had with the third one, the day-to-
day thoughts have made way for regret.

I really screamed at her. She was looking for her cellphone,
stressing, and then she started shouting at everyone while I was
in the middle of clearing the dinner table. At first I didn't react,
but then she came closer, talked louder, said something accusing,
loud, spoiled, sassy, and intolerable. And in one second, I snapped.

I surprised both of us. I shouted and said terrible things. I
told her that she can't shout like that and that I was sick and
tired of . . . there was a long list of things that had nothing to do
with her that I must have been really sick and tired of because I
shouted all of them. She burst into tears. I slammed the door of

the fridge and turned around to wipe the kitchen counter. We didn't look at each other anymore. The house was silent even though we were all there, all seven of us; silent apart from my shouting. Standing beside the sink, her sister turned around to me and said, "Enough, Mom." And the word *Mom* finally brought the episode to an end, reminding me of my role, so I shouted that I was going to take the little one to bed and for everyone to be quiet. I didn't even look at her, leaving her in the kitchen, shocked and hurt.

After the little one fell asleep, I stepped out of the room and was "Mom" again. The racing heart and lack of control had dissipated. I went into the third one's room and found her getting her bag ready for school tomorrow. The moment before I said sorry, I was overwhelmed with the most terrible, awful sense of guilt. She looks big, talks like an adult, gets angry like a grown-up, but she's still my little girl, and I lost control and shouted at her like crazy and wouldn't even stop when she started crying. And I have no idea why or how it happened, and I'm so sorry. I apologize, I ask for her forgiveness.

When *sorry* is said genuinely, it has an almost paralyzing power. This strong word, when spoken sincerely, can truly heal pain, reconcile relationships, build trust. Saying sorry lets us come closer together, be more vulnerable, more human. Sorry helps us acknowledge subjectivity, the fact that each person has an entire world or personal logic of their own, with its unique sensitivities, pains, and interpretations. When one world meets another world, sometimes someone gets hurt, someone isn't fully understood, someone is in pain. There is so much strength in that moment, when one person acknowledges hurting another, without ifs or buts. Just saying sorry for having hurt another person. So why do we try to teach them to say this word automatically?

"Say sorry to your brother! Can't you see he's crying?" "Say sorry to your father and he won't be angry anymore." "A well-behaved child says sorry and thank you. Say sorry!" "You didn't really mean it—say sorry again and mean it." "Now let's ask him if he's forgiven you. Have you forgiven him?" How many times did we explain to them, at the very moment and place where the offense or wrongdoing was perpetrated, that they had to say sorry? It's basic, isn't it? But let's try to look at this important topic through our children's eyes.

Option number one: "I snatched his ball, now he's crying. I did something wrong. To fix it, I need to say one word: 'sorry,' and then everything will be okay again. So this word, which is relatively easy to say, especially if you're only paying lip service, erases the offense, and in five more minutes, when I feel like snatching the ball again, I'll just do it and then say sorry again."

Option number two: "I did something wrong that hurt someone and to balance things out I have to pay a price—to say (usually openly rather than intimately) in front of the whole kindergarten or Grandma and Grandpa or friends a word whose sole purpose is to humiliate me. So I said it, and now we're even, and we can move on."

Obviously, both options are problematic, and neither really acknowledges wrongdoing against another person. I'd like to raise children who will know other people's pain the way they know their own, who will be careful not to hurt others, who will steer clear of excuses and ideologies that permit hurting anyone else. But the way to achieve this is not by placing them in a humiliating position until they apologize but by letting them experience a genuine apology and letting them offer a proper apology when necessary.

Now, all the ambassadors of authoritative parenting will protest and say that this is exactly how you unravel the family hierarchy that preserves our authority. Parents shouldn't apologize to their children, according to this point of view, and if you do happen to apologize, then you have to explain immediately how you reached this situation and why they are by no means allowed to talk or behave the way they did.

I, on the other hand, claim that everything our children experience, see, and feel in their initial relationships in their family of origin, our family, they take along with them to other meaningful relationships in their lives. If they *experience* a genuine apology, then they might not feel so humiliated when someone tells them to say sorry and they might not think it's pointless when someone else apologizes to them. This can help them realize that saying sorry is often something that brings you closer to someone, not something you do just to feel sanctimonious; that it's a sign of strength, not of weakness; and that after a real apology, both sides feel better.

It might take some time until you hear a genuine apology from them, but the real goal isn't necessarily to bring them to apologize properly to you but mostly to let them feel what happens when that word is uttered from a clean place, leaving the ego out of it, without force, reproach, or rekindling the controversy. Our parental job is to model behaviors for everything we want, expect, and dream they will become, because there simply is no other way of teaching children.

— *fourteen* —

When Mom and Dad Fight

It's Saturday evening on the road on our way back from Grandma and Grandpa's. The sun is setting. Dad is driving, Mom is sitting beside him, and my brother Rani and I are nice and comfy in the backseat. The radio is playing an old tune and Rani is already fast asleep, his body stretched out. My eyes are trying to close, but I wait, keeping the sleep away so that it doesn't creep in too soon. It always happens when you drive at night and everything around is dark and pleasant. Mom and Dad chat, she laughs and taps the window with her right-hand fingernails to the beat of the music. I can tell by the melody of their conversation that it's coming, know every note in her voice and his so well, and then her left hand and his right hand meet. He drives with one hand, she gives him a quick glance, smiles. His finger, her finger, then his again, intertwining for a few seconds. Now I can shut my eyes.

Mom, Dad, the space between them—that's home. Or Mom and Mom, Dad and Dad, or any other family constellation. In this space, kids grow up, internalizing the relationship, deducing their own future relationship choices on its basis. Before we have kids, the way we fight doesn't contaminate anyone's world but our own. When the kids join our lives, thousands of little reasons that can justify thousands of arguments are created. The way we conduct these arguments will affect the level of pollution in which our children grow up. When we put on our war paint and head out to battle, they watch.

Every parent knows the room that opens up in their heart when they see their children playing together, hugging, laughing, or just chatting. The sense of security and success that good relationships in the house give us is intoxicating. On the other hand, when they fight and their hands start waving about, their shouting growing louder and jealousy rising to the surface, we intervene, balance, educate, and, most of all, worry and suffer.

Now try to think what happens to them when we fight. After all, they can't really intervene, decide that Mom needs a bit of a breather, come between their parents, or ask us not to talk that way because "in our house we don't talk like that." But have no doubt: take the worry and anxiety we feel when they fight, and double it. Every time the argument deteriorates to insults and loud tones, contempt and disrespect, they hear it; the fact that they look as if they are minding their own business, letting us shoot our arrows of venom at each other without interruption, doesn't mean that they don't mind. They are attentive to our volume, their hearts tell them to be quiet so as not to burden us too much, and their greatest fear is that the concrete situation of the argument won't end, that from now on they will grow up in hatred. Yes, hatred—this is what we're spreading right now. They put their heads down, dive deep, and pray for it to be over.

Fights and disagreements are part of life. Where there aren't any arguments and differences, there isn't a real relationship—remember that next time you jump up and preach to them while they're fighting. But how do you manage to argue properly when there are children in the house?

Try to imagine yourselves arguing in a restaurant, while out with friends, in the presence of your grandmother or parents. Try to conduct the argument with self-respect. Having a civilized argument doesn't mean you can't raise your voices, but it does mean you can't scream or lose control. Harsh things may be said, but not things whose sole purpose is to hurt the other. The crying, slamming of doors, your darkest thoughts—all those can stay out of your living space; keep them for the late hours of the night, a drive in the car without the kids.

Don't set the example of leaving the house in the middle of a fight, even if it's just for a short while. The last thing you want when they become teenagers is for them to leave the house in the middle of an argument. If they're young and seem worried, pause and explain: "I'm very angry at Daddy right now and we're arguing and trying to explain to each other how we feel. It's not pleasant to argue, but soon, when we're done arguing, we'll make up and it will be pleasant again."

Now let's focus on the arguments themselves, especially those related directly to the children. When we set out on the journey of parenthood, we meet our partner's style of parenting for the first time. It's not that we couldn't imagine what it would be like before the children were born, but the moment we become obliged to function as parents, we are almost always exposed to aspects of our partner's style of parenting that we never imagined. This often creates a split that establishes parental behaviors that are nothing but a response to the other's conduct. For example, if he is impatient, I'll jump up every time I believe his impatience is hurting the kids. Without noticing, I become much more patient just to counterbalance him. He in turn becomes even more impatient, because now he's not only impatient with the kids but also with me—impatient about *my* style of parenting.

Try to imagine your children talking about you, about your qualities. Even if they are only three years old, try to imagine them speaking as if they were twenty-year-olds. What would they say? "Mom always gives in. Dad always insists." "When I'm angry and crying, Mom always hugs me and Dad always gets angry right back." "When I screw up, Mom is very critical, so I only talk about my mess-ups with Dad." These sorts of sentences reflect roles that you have to switch from time to time, otherwise the kids will pay a heavy price. Not switching roles creates a good cop–bad cop scenario, which forces us into far more extreme positions than the ones we started off with.

Parents have to rely on their base of strength, on what comes naturally to them. If the parental role is serving the parents and the children well and everyone is happy, that's usually a sign that everything is working properly. But once in a while, we also have to make our methods of action more flexible; to be the good cop and the bad cop at the same time, impatient and the picture of patience, tough and soft, knowing and clear yet consulting and questioning. You don't want them to head out into life with an inner split between goodies and baddies, black and white, but with a profound richness that is the result of a clear upbringing offered by parents that have two distinct styles of parenting, common goals, and plenty of mutual respect. And when there are significant differences along the way, over the goals or the style, you just have to pull over, sit down for a board meeting, and recalculate your course.

Remember that the children also need to see you happy together. We're so busy raising them, driving them, arguing, delegating, finishing things, and putting out fires that we often seem, in their eyes, like roommates or factory managers. Those magical moments, the ones that will stay with them forever, are the ones in which your hands suddenly touch in the car, you hug in the kitchen while making supper, a hand rests on the other's back while watching TV, a little romantic smile passes between you, you kiss when you come into the same room, you snuggle up together in bed on a Sunday morning. Give your partner a piggyback ride, laugh and make them laugh, have fun, love, open the wedding album and laugh about how much hair Daddy used to have and about Mommy's dress with the exaggerated frills; tell them about how you fell in love, how exciting it was. It may be ancient history, but it's their story as much as it's yours, because they are the products of that love, and somehow, in daily life, they need to really witness it.

When a child is used to seeing her parents in a good relationship, she can sleep better at night even when they argue.

— fifteen —

The Stork's Visit

MY BROTHER RANI BURST INTO MY LIFE WHEN I WAS two and a half. My father picked me up from kindergarten and told me I had a baby brother. He put me in the backseat of the car to go to the hospital and took out a bar of chocolate from the glove compartment. He broke off four pieces, even though I was usually allowed just one piece, and said that today was a very sweet day, a day I'd remember even though I was still very young, because today I'd become a big sister.

When a new baby joins the family, it takes a few weeks to recuperate as parents and for the baby, which starts off as a little unphotogenic lump, to become more "defined." And then we stage the perfect photo—a little girl in a clean white shirt holding her new baby brother; such sweetness, such joy.

But there is also sadness in that moment of a child's life when a sibling is born, when they understand, genuinely understand, that this creature is here to stay, that the family map has changed and will never go back to being the way it was. She won't have her picture taken alone anymore, and even if she will—she isn't really alone. She has to part with being the only child, with the family portrait as she knew it, with herself as she knew herself, and she must now share a new life with someone new, who, with his entrance into the family, expelled her from paradise. The safest place in the world has moved, another little person with needs and demands for attention has joined, the roles have changed, the day-to-day reality has changed, and a worry arises, not as a concrete thought but as one that nevertheless becomes clear and present, just like in the game of musical chairs: the music is playing, everyone is circling the chairs, the music will stop in a moment, and I just might find myself without a chair.

I believe that siblings are wonderful gifts, but let's not expect our child—eldest, second, third—to feel the excitement and awe that we feel when a sibling comes along. Imagine your husband coming home one day with a young, beautiful, and incredibly sweet woman and saying: "Don't worry, I love you just as I did before. This woman will just sleep with me in our room and wear the clothes that are too small on you." Imagine your wife coming home with a strapping, tanned man who has a wonderful sense of humor and saying: "This is a big present I brought especially for you! You'll be best friends. From now on he'll come everywhere with us, and every time he makes a sound, we'll pay attention to him, because he is new. Oh, and would you mind taking a picture with him so we can brag about having another one?"

So, yes, try to take pictures of your eldest alone, too. Find a unique and special place for her, a room in your heart that belongs to her alone, where she can know that despite being cast out of paradise, she'll always be your love. Here are a few more things you can do.

Be Truthful

Don't make up stories or hide anything. You can buy him a present to celebrate the exciting event, and you can help him choose a gift from him for his new sibling or from you to him because you're very excited and the fact that he is now a big brother is a wonderful reason to buy a present, raise a toast, or even organize a party at kindergarten. Just check with him in advance to see what he would like most. It's the time to explain that he's big now and that you can consult him about things that could make him happy.

If you're planning a party to celebrate the baby's arrival, prepare your older child. Let him choose a dessert or a song to play at the party, a blanket for the baby, or a greeting that he can dictate and you can read out loud to the guests. Presents, sweet things, and parties are fun, but do it out of excitement and happiness for him and not out of a need to compensate or protect him. Don't wait until he is out of the house to kiss and snuggle your baby, because deep in his heart he'll know that's what you're doing. He needs truth, because everything is very complicated for him on the inside right now. He needs you to protect the baby, love it, and hug it, because through that he judges (in an indirect and unaware way) how much you love and protect him.

Parents really do love all their children   that should be his conclusion.

Have Patience

As parents we talked about it, prepared ourselves, and *chose* to bring another soul into our world and into the world as a whole.

But if you think that when you asked your other child "What's in Mommy's tummy?" and she said "A baby" it meant she understood, or when you read her books about it that she really felt what it would be like, or when her friend had a little sister that she could picture how it would be for herself—you're wrong.

Many months will pass—not as a result of her own choice and during which she has no control over anything—until the moment she really understands what it means to be a big sister and manages to communicate it. Time plays a major role in proving things will be okay, and the burden of proof is on you. Only when a sufficient amount of time has passed and you fulfill your parental role and prove that there is no chair missing in your game of musical chairs, that when the music stops she still has her own chair, that no one has really taken her place even if someone is sleeping in her baby bed, wearing the clothes that used to be hers, and feeding from her mother's breast—only then will she be able to express sadness, jealousy, and anger; regress; and initiate power struggles. Displaying these and other behaviors helps her understand the new situation, prepare herself—like how you had prepared yourselves—to really become a big sister.

Give Older Kids Privileges

Many parents say, "He's so wonderful with the baby—strokes him, shows him off to friends. He's just angry and more difficult with us. It has nothing to do with the baby." It has everything to do with the baby! You have a wise and sensitive child who realized from the very first moment that there is no reason to be angry at the little bundle in the crib. Furthermore, if he does get angry at the baby, he might be thrown out of the club.

So, what can a three-year-old do with the fear of losing his place that comes with the clarity that this new little creature is really important to his parents? The answer: he can *be angry*—if not at the baby, then at those who brought him along. And he can *try acting* little again and regress—because the grown-ups clearly prefer the little one. Or he can be annoying, whine, refuse to cooperate, and behave in ways that will get his parents to focus on him and give him attention. So, sympathize and relate being "big" with the cool things: "Only us big ones can talk, eat ice cream, read big boys' books, and climb up tall ladders on the playground."

Talk to the baby and make sure your older child can hear: "When you're as big as him, you can do it, but now it is absolutely out of the question!" Consult with him about the baby: "What shall we dress her in today?" "Shall we change her diaper now or hug her first?" "What do you think she's trying to say?" Give him grown-up chores that aren't related to caring for the little one: "You're so big and strong, so independent and grown up that we've decided to give you a grown-up's job   you'll be in charge of taking the mail out of the mailbox." Or in charge of bringing everyone glasses to the table or turning out all the lights when you leave the house. And at night, when you take him to bed, ask to tickle him like you used to tickle him when he was a baby, tuck him in the way you tuck babies in, play peek-a-boo—because he'll always be your baby too.

Quarreling Is a Privilege

I F YOU ASK ME, OR YOURSELF, WHAT YOU WOULD WISH for your children twenty years from now, somewhere in the top ten you'll find the sincere wish that they will have a good relationship with their siblings, that they will be able to count on each other, meet on weekends with their families, know that despite being different, the string that linked them together in childhood continues to connect them. So why on earth do they keep fighting all the time? What are we doing wrong?

When the second child is born, a new entity is born with it: the relationship between the children. From now on there is the older one, the younger one, and the relationship. The relationship that is born through the moments they share together every day—sitting in the bath, laughing together, or just eating side by side—fills us with unparalleled joy. We look at them and feel success. But when they fight? Then we immediately get into action and try to do everything we can—separate, blame, punish, shout, offer creative solutions ("Why don't you take turns?" "So you let her have it now and she'll let you have it later"), or tell them how disappointed we are in them. But the bottom line is that nothing helps. So here are a few things worth remembering.

You Don't Actually Know What They're Fighting About

When I fight with my husband in the evening because he didn't wash the dishes, and voices are raised and even some unpleasant words are spoken, I'm not really arguing with him about the dishes. I'm arguing with him because there is an imaginary memo pad in my heart that says he forgot our anniversary, didn't answer his cell, didn't tell me the day before yesterday that he loved me, and bought the brand of cream cheese that I hate at the supermarket. If a third person steps in and tries to judge this argument, they'll never know about the things written on this memo pad. Your kids also have little memo pads in their hearts, and you can be sure that there are plenty of things written there in an indecipherable writing that even they couldn't make out. In the siblings' department you might find things like, "My brother has it so easy"; "I'm sick of my sister taking all the attention the moment she walks into a room"; and "From the moment he was born, he has always been able to make Mom laugh" or "Why does everyone say he's just like Dad (and I'm not)?" All these open accounts, and wishes to be the one and only special one in Dad and Mom's eyes—any child's ultimate heart's desire surfaces when they argue, usually without them being aware of it. And we, who think we know each one of our children so well, neglect the third entity, the relationship, and intervene, usually crudely and without understanding the bigger picture.

You Don't Really Know Whose Fault It Is

Many of us fall into the trap of "You're older, so give in" or "Why do you always hit?" Don't hurry to categorize them and definitely don't share their assigned category with them. After all, the "poor" little one could use his two little legs to get away from his menacing big sister but chooses to stay in the fight and to call you to solve his problem.

When the shouts of "Moooommmyyy!" are heard, there's nothing better than staying in the other room and calling back, "I'm in the kitchen—whoever needs anything is welcome to come here." They usually don't come. The idea isn't to turn your back on them and say, "As far as I'm concerned, you can kill each other," but to let go in a way that clarifies that you trust them and their good relationship, that you know they are also supposed to fight, and that it's okay because they also know how to make up. "I won't intervene, I won't be the judge, I won't step into the room and ask 'What just happened here?' If they need some comforting after being insulted, I'll happily give a kiss and a hug. I'm right here. But I won't be dragged into 'tell him' and 'it's her fault' because the chances are that I won't know exactly what happened, how it all started, and whose fault it really is."

You Can Get the Message Across When It's Quiet

When they fight, shout, and cry, don't look at them with a disappointed expression, don't feel that you've failed, and don't get angry at them, because fighting is a privilege. Be the sponge, the container in which they can fight safely, and if it does deteriorate to violence (and no, ladies and gentlemen, a little push or tug isn't violence), you can stop the fight. We won't judge, we'll just tell them that if they are interested in fighting, they'll have to do it without throwing objects or pulling hair. And when we say such things, we will be sure to address both of them, putting them in the same boat, even if we think we know who was the one to raise their hand first.

No Need to Demand Apologies

When children make up, they don't need the word *sorry*. They just get back to playing, and they do it much faster if we don't get in the way. So give up on the "say sorry" and "do you accept his apology?" It's unnecessary. You can go over to them after they're playing again and say, "I'm so happy that you know how to forgive each other. You're such good people, such good siblings."

seventeen

"I Love You Even Though I Hate You"

M Y NINE-YEAR-OLD'S BIRTHDAY TABLE WAS PREPARED by her siblings after she went to sleep. Balloons were blown up, a pretty tablecloth was spread, and presents were arranged in the center of the table. Every sibling helped according to their ability and style: the seventeen-year-old carried the birthday things into the house, the fifteen-year-old filled the balloons with air, the twelve-year-old decorated the table, and the four-year-old fell asleep "thinking of a birthday greeting." I looked at them, busy with the birthday ritual I had instilled in the family routine, and thought how easily they were doing something for someone else and how important it is to raise children who can let someone else be in the spotlight and still feel helpful and useful. Maybe because everyone looks forward to the cake that will be waiting for them in the morning, maybe because each sibling is expected to congratulate the birthday boy or girl, and maybe because they know that the day will come when the table will be set with special presents especially for them.

The next day, right after the candles were blown out, we had a family dance and got over the four-year-old's tantrum before getting around to the birthday messages. The older ones had already learned how to deliver a special message: they started by commending the birthday girl's good qualities, then addressed their relationship with her or the things they like to do with her, and finished off with wishes for the coming year (which are usually things they wish for themselves). When it was the little one's turn, he said: "I love you, Rona, even though I hate you."

Negative emotions are an inseparable part of the range of emotions we feel every day. We feel anger, jealousy, and hate just as we feel joy, pleasure, and satisfaction. The older our children get, the more we have to realize that our heart's desire of "just don't let her get hurt, be sad, be offended, fail, or get her heart broken" is misguided. As parents, we are supposed to hold on to that hope but, at the same time, allow our children to handle all the negative emotions life has to offer, especially within the family environment.

The home is a microcosm of everything we will think about the world. In the home, we learn without words what a man, a father, a woman, a mother, a relationship is; what love feels like; what rejection feels like; what it means to be together or alone; who *I* am and who *they* are. Our subjectivity as human beings stems from these relatively few years of learning, failing, succeeding, and, most of all, experiencing relationships. During these wonder years, the brief time we spend with our family of origin, we feed off the most significant oxygen supply life can give: intimate relationships with people who aren't going anywhere.

The beauty of good family relations is that they don't include a feeling of abandonment, and so they create one of the most significant training fields for children. There, in the relationship with siblings who are equal to them, they learn negotiation; the difference between weak and strong, pleasant and unpleasant, fighting and making up; they learn compromising and living together. The most important message in the family is that, for better or for worse, we are all committed to living with each other, to creating a pleasant place, and no less importantly, to being unafraid if things get less pleasant.

If, in the time they spend with us, children encounter negative emotions and know how to contain them as part of life, they will go out into the world and not crash every time they feel defeated, angry, or sad. We can give them the greatest human survival gift of all: the ability to be in an intimate relationship and not freak out the first time they have a negative thought about their partner; to work in a competitive environment without feeling as if someone else's success comes at their expense; to survive being let down by a close friend and to be able to talk to her about it; to contain pain and disappointment without feeling as if it's the end of the world, without developing a victim complex that makes them blame the world for their bitter fate. So why do we get so worried when they are unhappy? Why are we so quick to fix things for them and take away disappointments? Why is it so painful for us when they come across emotions that are supposed to prepare them for life, build their strength, develop important tools for their happiness?

Maybe siblings come along exactly because we are not very capable in this department. Facing each other, they are going to encounter every negative emotion the universe has to offer, and our job will be to not get in the way. We just have to look on from the sidelines and be thankful for this training field, even if it does at times feel like a battlefield. And when they suddenly behave differently, we should ask them how they managed to get over the jealousy, hate, or anger and show them how much power they have when they manage to feel such an irritating feeling and still get past it to find happiness or a solution or pleasure.

Let's not hurry to make them feel bad every time they have negative feelings toward each other. But let's not be afraid to name these emotions: "You are angry right now. I understand it's making you sad, because you'd also like shoes like these/a party like this/a characteristic like this and you feel jealous. You know, I was also jealous of my brother when he did well at school without even studying, while I always had to do my homework because I knew I just didn't have it as easy as he did." If we tell them that even we, who are already grown-ups, sometimes have these feelings and try to get over them, maybe we'll manage to train them to know what they feel and to be able to communicate it. To be able to acknowledge the fact that it is an unpleasant emotion, but it's okay. They might get to know themselves better and love themselves even when they are not at their best, and maybe they'll grow to love others when they're not at their best either. These are human emotions, and there isn't any need to invest so much energy in erasing or blurring them.

If we don't panic, they can learn that despite the stormy emotions that exist inside them, they are still running the show of their own lives and can choose the impact they are going to allow these emotions. They can accept the fact that negative emotions toward others and themselves might be unpleasant, but they are part of life, and thanks to their ability to contain those emotions without getting alarmed, they will also know what they need to do to overcome them.

We experience the strongest negative emotions when we face those closest to us, and for good reason. The mother who manages to accept the negative emotions she can feel toward her own children is a better mother. But to achieve this, we must recognize the fact that we are imperfect and that we can't really make our children happier if they don't know themselves in unhappy places too.

Think for a second about all the grown-ups you know. Think of the ones who attack the moment anyone gets angry at them. They can't handle the feeling that someone is angry at them, and then they protect themselves in the most inefficient, alienating way there is: by lashing out. Think about the ones who get insulted and immediately label the insulter as mean or wrong or erase him from their lives and break all contact. Think about those who don't maintain steady relationships because the moment the feeling of falling in love passes and they come across other emotions, they mistakenly think they must continue to search for "the one" with whom they will feel purely happy and good. Think about those who quit every time their boss is displeased or when they feel they are lacking a pleasant, significant feeling, who then assume that they are unappreciated or in the wrong profession. Think of those who can't voice all the terrible emotions they feel toward themselves, which leads them to shut people out because they believe no one can understand or contain what they are feeling. Think about all the unhappy people, the self-pitying, angry, and embittered people you know.

It very well may be that someone in their distant past didn't let them feel okay even when they were feeling bad; feel loved even when they expressed negative emotions; feel whole even when a flawed emotion seeped out. Someone didn't let them love someone despite—and perhaps because of—hating them at the same time.

eighteen

No Ordinary Greeting

O N MARCH 7 IN DELIVERY ROOM 6, AFTER AN eighteen-hour stillbirth, I realized for the first time just how much good luck you need. "From now on, when I pray, I'll ask for good luck," I thought to myself, suddenly gaining a profound understanding of this wish, like a real epiphany.

Our child's birthday is a day on which we remember our own good fortune and congratulate the birthday child for their good fortune. This is the day our children wait for every year. There are birthday activities and sparkling presents, sound systems and inflatable playgrounds, supplemented by numerous celebrations— at kindergarten, after-school day care, and ballet or judo class. For you, this can be tiring and replace the real joy with a long list of chores and errands.

The event that should be the most important one to you— and if you market it this way, it will become the most important part for your children—is the morning of the birthday, the real day your child was born and you were born as parents, the day you will always celebrate (and by the way, it makes no difference if it's your first or fourth child—with every child a different parent is born within us). On this morning, we don't need more than fifteen minutes to tell the child's birth story (not focusing on the epidural or traumatic delivery but on how we dreamed of him or her, how we imagined them, how thrilled we were with them) and hold a short ceremony when everyone, including siblings, offers their own birthday wishes. We can join together for a family hug and hear her make a little wish. You can also add a present, but as they grow older what they will remember is the love and support of their family.

Children know how to communicate from a very young age, but it doesn't mean that they realize the significance of a birthday, even if you did explain it to them. A noisy, busy celebration that is focused on them doesn't make the significance any clearer. From about four, you can sit with a child and ask them how they would like to celebrate. The process when a child is young is like a guided imagery exercise: What will it look like? Who will come? Where will it be? What will we do? Just think in advance what sort of options you'd like to describe so that you don't find yourself searching online for purple ponies because that was what came into her mind while you were talking.

But, please, listen to your child: if he's shy, maybe he doesn't feel like an event with lots of guests; if she's sensitive to noises or crowded places, maybe offer something fun with the close family; if he has stranger anxiety, think about an activity you can organize yourselves rather than bringing in the professionals.

Although you want to get it done in the fastest, most efficient way, let her help. A child who actively helps to organize her birthday party—decorating the cake, inflating balloons, or preparing the surprise bags—gains a sense of control that reduces her level of anxiety. The most difficult moments are those of waiting for the guests to arrive, so it's best to keep her occupied at that time, no matter if you ask for her advice about where the folding table should be placed or get her to fill the bowls with snacks.

Even after all the preparations, both the physical and emotional, there might come a point when it's just too much for him. He might cry or throw a tantrum. Maybe because he was too excited before it started, maybe because he has had enough after half an hour, maybe because he's just too young. Don't be upset—for yourselves or for him—and don't try to remind him about all the agreements you made beforehand. Just understand him, hug him, and even whisper in his ear, "When will everyone leave already?" and most of all, remind him and yourself just how much you waited to hear the sound of him crying when he was born. Ask him humorously to cry a little on every birthday, because that's a big part of the celebration.

Just don't lose your heads! I often think longingly about simple number-shaped cakes (3 or 4, which is actually the hardest to make), covered with frosting and tasteless sprinkles that get stuck between your teeth. One candle, a big puff, and a song. I don't have a problem with fondant icing, but I'm less partial to the "most imaginative cake competition," the feeling that if I make a three-layered cake that unites Elsa with Hello Kitty at the top, it means I'm a better mom. A child who decorates her own cake might have more fun, and besides, the candle is what really counts.

Putting a candle on the cake is an old tradition that originated in ancient Greece, when the cake represented the moon and the candle its glow. When a child blows out the candle and makes a wish, the smoke from the candle goes up into the sky and the wish comes true. Tell your child that she is your wish that came true, that she was in your dreams while you blew out candles all those years, that the smoke that went up with your wish actually worked. Look at her while she closes her eyes, just before she blows out her candle, and see your wish make a wish.

nineteen

The Child You Don't See

ONE DAY, WHILE I WAS SEARCHING FOR AN IMAGE ON my phone, I found myself going over lots of photos of my children at the playground, in the swimming pool, and at various other summer activities that a family with five kids does. The youngest one took the lead in appearances, leaving her siblings lagging. For the past three years, the one glued to my breast was also the one who appeared in a multitude of sweet images every time I touched my screen. Same with my screen saver. But three others shared the silver and bronze. And then it hit me—one of my children, the second one, simply wasn't there.

The reason the second child wasn't photographed isn't because he refused to have his picture taken, and it wasn't because he was going through a less photogenic period, either. He was with us on all the family outings. The reason his picture wasn't taken is because he had become a blur—I had lost my focus on him. He flew under my radar, and the others took his place. He didn't make any dramas and he was always just fine. He didn't get his picture taken because I didn't see him.

I continued to browse through the photos and a flash of insight hit me about why we were having such a hard time with him in the last month: he was busy making an effort to become visible, a hard task for a young child. He could have invested his energy in many positive things but was instead engaging us with a range of annoying and creative naggings that, at the end of the day, were making him intolerable. A see-through child, even if you feed him, buy him clothes, read him stories, ask him how his day went, will still recognize that he comes last in your stream of photographs and will do everything to become your screensaver.

A child needs the feeling that he is being seen, that the whole of him is being seen all the time. When he is sad or successful, when he's having a hard time or an easy time, when he clams up and when he opens up; to see the nuances in the corners of his mouth, the eyes, the tone, the intentions, his dreams and fears. And by the way, the fact that you're required to *see* really doesn't mean that you're required to fulfill his every need all the time. Seeing alone, the feeling that *I exist, belong, am loved and visible*, is the main thing in a child's experience and sense of self-worth. Children who are clearly seen, without criticism or judgment, without competition or comparisons, grow up to be adults who can see themselves through positive lenses and can see others, too, and make room for them.

The problem is that the parental eyes sometimes see things a little too clearly and judge: she's not developing fast enough, he doesn't look handsome enough, he doesn't have enough friends, she isn't learning properly, she teases her brothers, he speaks impolitely, he eats too much, he eats too little, she's lazy, she doesn't initiate things. And there are also the eyes that have a blurry vision, missing the things that are either hidden or out in the open; and there are the eyes that worry that something is wrong, the eyes that fear. These eyes need glasses to slightly change the perspective, filter out the unnecessary, remove or tone down the judgment, and especially, sharpen what really counts. Just as we wear our sunglasses when the sun is too strong and then see things a little more easily.

One of the difficulties involved in the way we see our children is related to the fact that we view them through two pairs of glasses: the first is the one we use to see ourselves, judge and manage the reality of our lives, and the second is the pair we put on the day we become parents. There lie our fantasies about what kind of children we want to have, how they will look and behave, what they will be good at, what our relationships with them will be like, and what sort of parents we will be. You're wearing two pairs of glasses, one on top of the other; you really can't see very well.

How can we see the picture a little differently, a little more clearly, and most of all, in a more complimentary light? Because, yes, we're all really good at seeing what's missing, we believe it's our job, but the lenses that show us what *is* there are healing lenses. So when one of your kids sneezes in the other room, shout, "Bless you, sweetheart!" or when your daughter is keeping herself busy, say "I see you're drawing and really enjoying yourself"; when someone remembers to put one of his workbooks in his backpack, even if he's forgotten the other seven, say "I see you remembered to take your literature workbook—that's called being responsible"; and if your annoying adolescent finally manages to wake up on time, say "I see you got yourself up on time, and it's really nice I didn't have to argue with you about it this morning."

It's important to remember that focusing on "other people's children," also known as "we are really screwed" or "why is our grass not as green?" creates an especially dangerous pair of glasses. "Why are all the other children sitting quietly in their strollers while their mothers are drinking coffee, and my little one is screaming?" "Why are all the other little girls thin, while my daughter looks twice their size?" "Why are all the other boys going out, and our son is staying in with us?" "Why are all the other children joining in on the activity, but she's just sitting in my lap the whole time?" Let's admit it: this focused zoom-in starts off with self-pity and ends with anxiety that leads to anger and aggression, which come out on our kids. It comes from the best intentions, of course—to turn your child into the neighbor's child: greener, stronger, prettier, more polite, and more sociable. But it doesn't help, and not because the grass is always greener on the other side, but because you're insisting on wearing glasses that are showing you a false image.

When you zoom out, you can see that in the greater scheme of things, the child who sits quietly in the stroller might have a hard time doing something else; the girl who joined in on all the afternoon classes might not manage to make a career for herself; the neighbor's beautiful boy might have severe learning disorders; and the child who sleeps through the night might be socially isolated in the eighth grade. And it's not because there's karma and everything balances out in the end, but because the whole is larger than the sum of its parts, and in each person and child there are weaker and stronger sides; and who said that you had to be one way or the other to pass the qualifying test?

There is nothing worse for a child than not passing his own parents' qualifying test, to see his father look admiringly at the neighbor's son and to hear his mom complain that he does nothing but play Legos. Unreasonably high expectations can have a devastating impact on our kids' self-image. So look at them really hard, even when it isn't easy, and see that now is just a pinpoint on the timeline of life. Their life.

twenty

The One Who's Never Happy

"WHY ARE YOU ALWAYS UNHAPPY? WHY DOES EVERY fun day have to end with a sense of deprivation? How did I raise a girl who makes a point of emphasizing everything that's flawed, doesn't work out, or goes wrong? It's called being ungrateful. And the worst thing is that you're going to have a very difficult life. Because if now, when everything is still relatively simple, you can't find one good thing to focus on, what will happen when life really hits you? How will you climb out of the deep holes with such a negative approach, seeing every tiny hollow as an abyss? What will become of you?!"

I'm saying all these sentences in my head, standing in front of her, just another normal day, not saying a word. I'm holding back, but everything is raging on the inside, and I feel a strong urge to just pour out all my frustration on her. How could it be that I raised a pessimistic child in my house? A child who feels deprived, who doesn't manage to be even marginally optimistic? Maybe if I set her straight, if I share all my fears, maybe then she'll realize that she's missing out, big time, that she has to learn to stop focusing on all the things she's missing.

But the most painful thought suddenly dawns on me: right now, in my thoughts and fears, I, myself, am focusing on what's missing. I'm also responding, just like her, to an unwanted reality. Her unwanted reality: she can't find her earphones and is going around the house screaming that her life is shit. My unwanted reality: looking at her behavior and thinking, "I have a messed-up child who needs to be set straight, needs to be fixed, needs to hear a piece of my mind so that she understands." So, just like her, I'm focusing on what's not working. I'm also feeling deprived, disgruntled, having a hard time being optimistic. How can I actually teach her? How can I create something else for her?

One of the most agonizing realizations in parenthood is that we taught them the opposite of what we had intended to teach them, out of the best of intentions, of course. The understanding that our reactions, which were supposed to eradicate a faulty mechanism, only reinforced it.

Our children come across many positive and pleasant experiences in their day-to-day lives, but they also encounter many situations in which their heart's desire crashes against the wall of life, like the last porcelain plate in a Greek *taverna*. We, as parents, realize that they aren't supposed to be content all the time and that to develop an anger and crisis management system, a child inevitably needs to encounter anger and crises. We also realize that the more developed they become, the greater the crises. A five-year-old can crash after a fantastic day if the last stop doesn't include chewing gum in the flavor she wanted. Try to imagine yourself at the end of a day when you took off work, met a friend for a coffee, took a midday nap, ate at a nice restaurant, and when you got home after all that, you found that someone broke into your house. Are you going to manage this crisis with cosmic optimism while keeping in the front of your mind all the positive sensations from your day of fun? So we can't really expect a child to stop everything the moment she experiences a crash, hold back her rage, and say, "Actually, Mom, I had such a wonderful day that I choose not to get upset right now and even to thank you for all the effort you made throughout the day to make me happy."

Why are we so convinced that they are being spoiled or ungrateful when it happens to them? Worse yet, why do we tell them that's what we think? What can they do with that allegation to improve the way they cope with the next disappointment? After all, "if Mom and Dad tell me that I don't know how to see the glass half full, they're probably right, I probably am ungrateful, or don't know how to cope, or am making a mountain out of a molehill. So this is what I know about myself, this is me." And this is how an inability to cope is born.

Often, the child with the biggest sense of deprivation in a family is the child who, according to her parents, gets the most. This means that the deprivation mechanism is working well for her and is managing to take over most of the family resources: "If we just give her enough, she'll say it's enough or feel it's enough. And when we give and give and she's still discontent, we tell her off and explain how she's never satisfied." And that's exactly how we reinforce the mechanism from both directions.

In fact, we should be thankful for every situation in which our children encounter life. We should be a little happy about them being displeased, because that's a sign that they are dealing with a complicated mission, encountering a hardship, feeling it, and, after coping with it, gaining the ability to mark it on a scale of proportion and maybe even to acknowledge the fact that, despite the hardships, life is pretty beautiful. So how do we help them?

~ When they are in the midst of a frustrating experience, don't expect them to be content or to be able to appreciate all the good things that happened before.

~ Understand the difficulty. Not in a condescending way. Remember that when they feel understood, their level of anxiety decreases and they have more emotional tools available for coping. Just understand them without saying "But it's just chewing gum" and without criticizing, without focusing on yourself and how they are wrecking your day right now.

~ Don't offer solutions. When we offer solutions, remove obstacles, and fulfill wishes just to avoid frustration, just to make sure they have a perfect experience, we feed the deprivation mechanism. We naturally want to create positive experiences for them, but there is a point at which we start feeling the sense of excessive giving. That's exactly where you have to let life speak, because even if we do go back to collect what we accidentally left behind or drive all the way to the special shop where they sell rainbow-colored popsicles, another frustrating stop will turn up. Why? Because it's hard to let go of a perfect day, hard to come back down after a positive experience, difficult to be tired but contented when deep inside you know that the fun is over, the day is over, the ice cream is finished, and you have to say goodbye to all these good things, go home, take a shower, and get into bed.

~ Offer a positive role model. A parent who recognizes and understands the hardship without falling apart and who is able to say to himself and to his crushed child, "It's really such a bummer that we couldn't find the popsicle you wanted. I know how annoying it is. I'm so lucky that I had such a lovely day with you. I love you also when you're not happy and I'm trying to remember now just how happy we were an hour ago, and that's making me feel a little better." This creates a model for raising optimistic people. And when they're happy, and they often are, take ten seconds to tell them what happy people they are, what experts they are in creating happiness, tell them that it's called being optimistic, and that optimistic people are really, really strong, because they know how to go on being happy even when unpleasant things happen. And that's real strength. And when something in your life goes wrong, remember that it's an excellent opportunity for them to act as audience and see that it happens to everyone, that it's normal. Call them over, ask them to cheer you up, to help you get over it. See how they remind you of the good things, learning how to encourage others, and you'll be moved by their ability to find happiness in places of anger, frustration, and sadness.

It takes time to learn how to manage anger. It takes years to familiarize yourself with the internal mechanism of cheering up and finding joy in times of hardship. Our job is to see the baby steps they are taking, not to get confused or to confuse them with frustrated, negative remarks. When they are lying in bed, submissively accepting the end of another day passed, whisper in their ear at least three wonderful things that happened to you with them that day. Release the part in you that feels the need to scold or threaten, the motivational talks, and the educational lectures about the optimistic child, and just be optimistic yourself.

twenty-one

Agreements with Children:
The Fine Print

I WAS PLAYING IN THE SANDBOX WITH A FRIEND, TWO seven-year-old girls, on summer holiday in Haifa, at a time when you didn't need adults to chaperone you. When we left the sandbox and walked toward the swings, I noticed that my mother's wedding ring was gone. It must have slipped off my tiny finger into the sand, mocking the promise I had made to myself only two hours earlier: "to take care of it, not to leave the house with it, to place it on the wooden nightstand beside my mother's bed whenever I wasn't playing with it. To understand and respect that the ring was very dear to her."

The promise broken, I, a child in the second grade, kneeled on all fours in the sandbox, using my fists as tiny shovels. My heart was pounding, my chin quivering, the grains of sand refusing to cooperate. My friend eventually went home, and I would have to go home and explain to my mother that I had lost her wedding ring.

We want to raise children who know that promises should be kept and that agreements must be honored, but how many times a day do we make agreements with our children that fall apart? It usually starts with some "no" we say, which is immediately followed by an exhausting and determined negotiation. And we, who suddenly seem to forget why we said no in the first place, offer the brilliant solution: "I'll give you another candy now if you promise not to ask for any at all tomorrow." "You can watch television now if you promise to wake up on time tomorrow by yourself." Just this week I overheard a mother at the playground making an agreement with her son: she would let him climb up on the tall wall and he, in return, had to promise not to fall.

Can a four-year-old really make a promise pertaining to the future, especially one that comes at the expense of his wants at that future moment? And if he doesn't manage to honor the agreement, which was sealed at a particular moment when he was willing to sell his own mother and father for another candy bar, what does that say about him? And what does it say about us parents, our boundaries, if every time we come across dissatisfaction, we're willing to replace our verdict with an agreement that will give us some peace and quiet in the next five minutes? If we want to teach our children that agreements are important and valuable, how do we avoid the classic traps that only lead them to conclude that we can't count on them?

The significance of an agreement with a child is that the parent cuts the child some slack when it comes to a boundary (sweets, screen time, fun time, schedule, and more) and the child, in return, offers a promise that in principle signals that she too is making her own compromise. The parent gives independence and the child gives responsibility. This is at the core of the conflict between parents and children, and it appears in full force in adolescence, when adolescents demand independence but have a hard time showing responsibility, while parents demand responsibility but have a hard time allowing independence.

Before children reach adolescence, they pass through a tender age, and when we're dealing with something tender we have to be careful not to squash it. Youngsters possess no abstract understanding of past–present–future, and so they have no real ability to plan an agreement. When there is a sweet, gift, screen, or any other pleasure at stake, they will talk to us using the language of agreements, but emotionally they won't be able to live up to it. We must live up to it for them, because we agreed; we should do this without anger, just by reminding them that this was the agreement.

Because we want to bring them in contact with their ability to honor agreements, we have to understand the skills our children must possess to do that. For example: being responsible, knowing how to restrain themselves, compromising, deferring gratification, being empathetic, and many other qualities. Before you know for sure that your child has all these abilities, you have to ask yourself whether the expectation that they honor the agreement is even vaguely realistic. For a child to be willing to honor an agreement, which will also deprive him of something particular, he needs to know that he has all the necessary qualities in himself to make it possible, and he needs a lot of positive reinforcement and a clear knowledge that it's all worthwhile. Every time you see so much as a glimpse of these qualities, you have to tell him how responsible he is, how well he resisted, how much you trust him. Just think how rarely a child hears that someone trusts him, and how that could influence his ability to trust himself.

And of course, there's nothing better than setting an example: instead of explaining it to your child, show her. Start off with silly agreements where only you pay the price. For example, make an agreement that you'll take them to the swimming pool or bring a surprise home for them or won't come home too late. Seal it with a handshake, as if they were also committing themselves to something. And then—honor the agreement. On the way to the pool, tell them it was really lucky that you made that agreement, because even though you didn't really feel like going to the swimming pool, thanks to the agreement, you're in the car on your way. Introduce them to a reality in which it's not always convenient to honor agreements but really fun to keep them, because keeping a promise has its own value, which is often more important than convenience or pleasure.

When you feel your child is ready to practice, introduce him to an agreement with a proximate outcome. For example, "I'll let you see the end of the program, but the moment it ends we take a bath." And then when he protests, cries, gets annoyed, or tries to make a new agreement, simply take him to the bath. Don't get angry, don't say "we can't trust you." Just help him take that bath empathetically and assertively. When you're done, even if it wasn't a very pleasant experience, wrap him up in a towel and whisper to him that it was really amazing that he kept his side of the agreement and let you bathe him.

Every time you know for sure that she's making that promise right now because she really wants something, but tomorrow or in a week's time, when you come to claim your part of the bargain, she won't actually be able to honor it (mostly because younger children are lacking the cognitive ability to see the abstract, and the present is the main thing)—decide for yourself whether you really want to offer a loan to someone who has no money. Guard the limit where it's important to you, give in when it's not really that important. Remember that when they, our little ones, shake hands and agree, they really want to honor the agreement and have the full intention of doing so, just like when we say to ourselves "Tomorrow we're starting that diet" or "We won't get angry again when they take too long in the morning." Just as we don't always follow through with promises we make to ourselves, they don't either. It's human.

twenty-two

OMG, First Grade!

A LETTER ARRIVES WITH THE SIX-YEAR-OLD'S NAME written on it. It's waiting in the mailbox: a special letter in a mundane pile of mail. It's an invitation to meet the child's new teacher, an invitation to first grade. A toffee is glued to the letter and Mom is excited as she reads it out loud. They sit by the kitchen table, his legs still not reaching the floor, and he swings them back and forth as he detects his mother's unusual excitement. There's also an unfamiliar sadness about her. She hugs him and tells him he's so grown-up and she can't believe that her third child is already going to school and that it's great that his teacher's name is Alona, because it's a lovely name and she's probably really nice. The child unwraps the toffee, puts it in his mouth, and as he chews it, the pieces sticking to his teeth, he thinks: "I wonder if my feet will reach the floor when I'm sitting in class."

A few months later, wearing a nice new shirt and carrying a schoolbag that feels really big, he walks through the gates of school, holding on tight to his mother's hand. The night before, they held their family ceremony. His mother wrote his name on a white plate with honey and he licked it all up. Dad explained that, like the sweet taste of the honey letters in his mouth, so the year ahead will be sweet with all he will learn. His mother's hand feels confident and he knows that very soon the hand will let go and he will stay with the schoolbag, the shirt, the new children, and the sweet taste in his mouth from last night.

Welcome to school. It's not clear who's more excited, us or them, but it's definitely a different kind of excitement. We realize that the years in kindergarten are over, that this little boy, who just two months ago was entitled to play games, sit on a small chair, enjoy unrestricted movement in space, stories, songs, and a play doctor's office in the corner, is stepping into a new world. A world in which he will sit by a table without making noise, where there are "musts" and order, a world with short recesses, where he needs to meet new friends, find the way to the schoolyard, and no longer feel scared of the ruckus and the older children. It is a new world of grades, workbooks, pencil cases, and homework. A world in which the restrooms are at the end of the hall and there are no longer any little towels or inviting colors on the walls. How will he find it? How will he make friends? We worry how he will react when he raises his hand and the teacher doesn't see it. When he can't find the right book in his bag. When he misses us.

The children are also excited. They realize that kindergarten is over. They did have a goodbye party at kindergarten, after all, walked with the other grown-up kids wearing a funny hat on their heads, got a photo and a card, had their picture taken with their teacher. For months we've been talking to them excitedly about the transition, about how big they are. But they are heading toward an experience that is still unfamiliar to their little bodies. The anticipation isn't for something familiar, but for something unfamiliar, and with all the excitement surrounding it, it's a bit of a load. They can't really explain it with words, not even to themselves, but they feel a little weighed down, and a little scared.

So, besides all the practical preparation tips, it's also worth thinking about the more complex emotional aspects. We have a tendency, which begins in the first years of kindergarten, to have a discourse with the children where the word *fun* repeats itself forty times a minute. When we go to see the school: "You'll have so much fun here!" "Look, there are swings here. What fun!" "You'll learn how to read—it'll be such fun!" "We'll buy you a binder that has a picture of Messi on it. Won't that be fun?" "You'll get to know new friends. Such fun!" Later, when they come back from kindergarten or school, we can't understand why our question "How was your day?" gets a one-word robotic and flat response: "Fun."

To prepare our children for the transition, we have to accept the fact that it's not going to be nothing but fun. Usually, the things we are worried about get buried in late-night conversations with our partners. In front of the children, we put on a little bit of a façade. So, sure, you don't need to share your fear that they won't make any friends, that the teacher won't be able to handle their ADD, and that it will take them two years to master writing the letter *A* properly. Start talking about your own excitement, tell them about yourself as a child: how it felt scary at first, how the school building seemed so big and gray, how the teacher didn't smile all the time and sometimes even shouted when one of the children misbehaved. Tell them that it was a little scary at first to step out into the long corridor and make your way to the schoolyard, how it took you a long time until you remembered the names of all the children in the class. Tell them that on the first day, when your mother or father walked you into the classroom and the teacher said, "Now all the parents have to leave the classroom—say goodbye," you even cried a little.

Also tell them about the things that *were* really fun: the school trips, the teacher with the funny voice, the secretary's office where you could make phone calls. Tell them about the new things you learned, the exciting feeling when the letters turned into words and then sentences—and you could read. The bell that everyone waited for, the school ceremonies, anything that you can remember.

The technical preparations are also an excellent opportunity for emotional preparations. Don't be tempted to order the books in advance, wrap them two months earlier, buy an especially elegant pencil case, and complete it all with a purple schoolbag by a famous brand. Put your own preferences aside, at least some of them, and in return you will get a child that will accompany you in this process and begin to feel part of everything that's going on. She'll be more in control by choosing, planning, trying to imagine what it will be like to be there with the schoolbag she has just picked, with that sticker on the workbook, which might be a little crooked, but hey—"I stuck it on myself"—and the letters of her name that will be written on all the notebooks and workbooks.

By including them, we give them a little more certainty, allow them to think and share their thoughts with us without any pressure, just while we're doing something pleasant that is supposedly a mere practical thing, and this is why it's so rewarding. Suddenly, all the notebooks and pencils that they put in the pencil case with their little hands transform into transitional objects, a hello from home, from themselves, from places where they have

control, and these objects will be there with them when everything is new and unfamiliar.

Before they start college, read this chapter again, and right
after you get over the feeling of how fast life flashes by, do what
you did so well before they started school and don't promise
them it will be pure fun. The honest discourse about fears, hardships, worries, excitement, and, yes, also fun, opens up an inner
dialogue with the whole range of emotions. And when there is an
inner discourse and there is someone to talk to, everything is a
little less scary.

twenty-three

Growing a Backbone

ELF-CONFIDENCE—WHAT IS IT AND HOW DO YOU RAISE a child that has some? As parents, how do we give them a boost while helping them keep their feet on the ground; make sure they know their own worth, know what they're good at, believe in their abilities; love themselves, project love onto the world, be positive because things are good? Wouldn't it be nice if someone could wrap the whole thing up and deliver it?

Somehow, in the first few years of their lives, this seems like an easy enough task: we adore them, tell them they are the smartest, funniest, most beautiful child; refuel them with our words. They believe us, and in seep the love and confidence; they walk around and the sun shines down on them. And then they encounter the world. In kindergarten, they start to suffer the pain that will later obtain different titles in their developing memory: "I was a very shy girl"; "All the boys were good at sports, but I wasn't"; "I was fat"; "I didn't have a lot of friends"; "I never drew very well." These labels are created in our absence, when we are not there to hug them or whisper encouraging words in their ears. They will be created in the company of children, with the kindergarten or school teacher, facing a world that is not in charge of their self-confidence.

Few children are born with a gift, a crown of light over their heads, beautiful and charming children who have the sun shining on them wherever they go, children the kindergarten teachers love, the ones all the other children want to befriend. My children are not like that. They are ordinary kids, ones who have to make an effort so that the mirror tells them good things about themselves. Not because they're not wonderful, beautiful, smart, or kind, but mostly because the world they encounter doesn't embrace them. They are not "the best"; they are themselves.

Assuming we are aware parents, we see the places where our children don't shine: fears, anxieties, shyness, pushiness, obsessiveness, inability to just go with the flow, possessiveness, and many other characteristics that have not yet fully formed. As they get a little older, we, who only a few moments ago knew without a shadow of doubt that they were "the best," suddenly start correcting, scolding, worrying, and getting disappointed. They look at us, because we are their mirror at this point, and see all the flaws. They look at us, unable to understand that we are angry or worried out of the best of intentions, that if they only listen to us and do as we say, they will succeed. They look at us and hear, "It's just this kind of behavior that will make other children not want to play with you" or "If you don't stop being so shy, you won't accomplish anything" or "So what if things aren't working out just the way you wanted? Just be more easygoing!" and "It's very unpleasant to be with you when you're angry. Until you calm down, nothing good will come of anything!" They listen to us and their fuel tanks empty, because now that they're having a hard time, we're putting them down even further, leaving them alone, taking away their confidence. They absorb our criticism, which is conveyed with a deadly mix of high expectations, anger, disappointment, and a lot of redundant words, and then they are supposed to go out and survive in the outside world, carrying within them their expulsion from our little paradise, the one that had accompanied them through the first years.

People with a positive self-perception develop self-confidence and self-esteem. Having that inner ability to know who we are and think well of ourselves helps us know and rely on our strengths. We often call this having a "backbone." It helps us stand firm in our beliefs and stand up for ourselves. Naturally, children or people who generally meet with success are ones whose ability to think highly of themselves is greater. But how many people like this do we actually know?

We are in charge of our children's story. We are the great storyteller, the narrator of their lives' adventures. Through this narrator's commentary and reactions to the hard parts, they will learn the "truth" that they tell themselves. The narrator can say: "You're a very brave child. Sometimes even the bravest people get shy or feel scared and insecure. I understand you when you feel shy. I'm sure that your courage will gradually help you overcome it when it's really important to you." Or the narrator could say: "You're acting shy again. Listen well: shy children are children who don't have any friends! They miss out on lots of good stuff! Shy children are the ones who don't get a surprise from the magician at a birthday party! Do you want to be that kind of child? Come on, get over it, because it can't go on like this." The thing that differentiates the two narrators is the point of view and the immediate interpretation that follows. They both watch the same show, but the optimistic narrator creates a different narrative to describe the weakness displayed. He doesn't blur it, but speaks about it from a place of acceptance, a place of understanding it as a developmental process that anticipates success and the ability to overcome obstacles. To create high self-esteem, we have to be an optimistic narrator for them.

And you know what? It starts by accepting ourselves as imperfect. When we can accept all our own flaws, the external and internal ones, we can speak about them with ourselves and the people close to us: "I know I'm really disorganized. I'm doing my best to improve." "I wish I exercised more, but it's hard to motivate myself." "I've got a really short temper. I try to be aware of it, rein it in, and apologize afterward." "I'd like to read more, but it doesn't always work out." When you are happy managing to meet some of your own expectations without criticizing yourself too much, you will have compassion. When you have compassion for yourself and can also express this to your children, they will learn compassion for themselves. Be with them when things don't work out because of a particular behavior or a mistake they made and when things annoy them, like the curly hair that they hate, and any other difficulty that they experience, and tell a different story: not "the best" story, but the story of "who you are."

If we want an easygoing child but going along with things doesn't come that easily to her, we have to identify the places where she does manage to be easygoing and get excited by them, just like the first time she clapped her hands. And when she doesn't, we should keep quiet, let her crash, and then hug her compassionately and whisper in her ear that today was hard and we saw how unpleasant it was for her. Maybe, just maybe, tomorrow it will be easier.

Teach your children to recognize the people who need a word of encouragement precisely when they are not at their best. Look at a child who's misbehaving at the playground, and instead of telling the regular story of good and bad, tell him that he's probably upset or having a hard time and needs a hug or a good word. Children who know that the world isn't separated into right and wrong, black and white, know compassion. Tell them that the thing that will make them happiest is to be good to others, to know how to listen, give a compliment, and put in a good word, especially when things are hard. People like that, children like that, are never really alone out there. When they look in the mirror, they will see themselves with compassion, know how to think well of themselves even when they are unhappy, and know how to see good in others and create goodness around them.

My son and I were walking down the street together when a phone call came, announcing that he had failed the summer exam. It was an important exam, because he had already failed twice and this time he was sure he had aced it. When he had emerged from the test, he had a big smile on his face, got into the car, and said, "I think I did really well this time!" So the announcement caught us off guard. He turned white. I could see he was making a real effort not to cry. I felt that a hug would hurt him, so I leaned next to him and remained silent with him for five minutes that felt like an eternity. He didn't say a word, just covered his eyes. And then I spoke into his ear. "You're my special boy," I said. "You're so smart and kind. You're turning into such an amazing man. And the most important thing is that you don't give up. That quality you have, not to give up, despite all the blows life hands you, is a winner's quality. I want you to remember what you can't feel right now: You'll win! Not because you'll pass some exam. You'll win because any other kid would have given up after two failures. I know many adults who would have given up after one, but you carried on. And even now, with your heart crushed, I know you'd never dream of despairing."

He didn't answer, just listened. I put my hand on his back even though I really wanted to hug him. "So which restaurant are we going out to tonight to celebrate your failure?" I asked. He laughed. We went on walking.

twenty-four

Their Homework Is
Their Homework

S HE CAME TO THE CAR WITH A SAD EXPRESSION, THE kind you don't often see on her face, she, a happy girl who always skips out of school, even if the schoolbag is especially heavy. I immediately asked what happened.

"A red X!" she cried. "That's what happened, Mom. Red Xs! Three!" The tears rolled down her cheeks as she bent over to take a crumpled piece of paper out of her schoolbag and straightened it out with angry gestures. She placed the math exam between us and pointed to another X and then another at the bottom of the page and then yet another. The Xs got a little smudged from her tears, as if turning into drops of blood. "A red X!" she repeated. "Why can't they just circle all the right answers? I'll already know that whatever isn't circled is wrong! Why do you need red Xs?"

How simple it would be if I could take away the pain of the X with just a sentence, a phone call to the teacher, an investigation of the event, or even a compliment. After all, they marked an X on my happy girl. Luckily for her, and for me, she isn't my first child and my motherhood has also been hurt often enough to know

119

one important thing: it's hers, this encounter with the Xs. Not mine. How complex is the realization that besides being there, besides understanding her and how she feels, besides the fact that I'm there to let her break down in the car, there's nothing much I can do. So I listened, I hugged, I put on a happy song, and when we got back home I circled the right answers and scattered a few hearts over the exam paper. She was already on her next life's mission, happy as usual, and I stopped for a moment and said to her: "I trust you. I love your crosses because they make you stronger. I love you because you're happy and clever and you overcome things." She smiled and went to do her homework.

Try to imagine a world of parenting that is without homework. No exams to prepare for or other school tasks. A world in which we take no part in the time management or the responsibility required in the field of schooling. A world where we only take interest in what they learned in history today, argue about a topic that came up in class, ask what letter they learned to write, or laugh about a word in French that rhymes with "snot." In this imaginary world, all the energy of the pressure we might put on them and the arguments over schoolwork is directed to encouragement and admiration: getting excited by a sentence they wrote nicely in their notebook; by them remembering by themselves that they have homework (as opposed to "Do you have homework? Are you sure you don't have homework? Shall I check?"); by seeing them take the initiative or ask for help with something that's proving hard (as opposed to "On Saturday we're going over square roots—you haven't really understood it.").

Understand, they can't really take responsibility when we're constantly proving to them that the person actually in charge of everything is us. We go on reminding them, sitting with them, correcting them, limiting the fun parts of the day and making them dependent on their completion of school tasks, fighting with them when they aren't concentrating and we're dying to get the homework over and done with. *Their* homework! And what for? The real goal is to teach them that it's their mission, that they have to invest energy, make an effort. If the person who ultimately makes the effort and takes responsibility is us, then what have we taught them?

Imagine yourself teaching your child how to ride a bicycle, and every time she loses her balance you quickly catch her, never letting her little feet meet the ground; you just straighten her up and give her another push. If she doesn't feel her own body's movements, if she doesn't comprehend the complexity of the mission—yes, you also have to hold on to the handlebars, pedal, keep your balance, and keep a steady pace—how will she ever learn? Worse yet, imagine that every time she falls—and she will fall, because that's what happens when you learn an independent task in life—you pressurize her, threaten, shout, say, "What's wrong with you—this is not how you ride a bike!" What will happen to her confidence, your relationship, her ability to take responsibility?

For a child to be able to take responsibility, we have to first believe that he can. Every time we take his homework out of his bag, hand him the pencil, and point to the next question, we prove the opposite. So let's take a deep breath and have faith in him. At first he just has to remember that he has homework and take the initiative to start on it by himself. We'll be impressed and say, "You remembered your homework without me having to tell you—you're becoming so responsible." When he takes the workbook out and opens it to the right page, we'll also be impressed. When he takes out a pencil from the pencil case, again we'll express enthusiasm. And when he sits and does his homework alone, allowing us to just be around doing something else, we'll tell him we appreciate his independence. When he says he doesn't want to do his homework now but later and we remind him later and he does sit down to do it—we'll tell him that that's all he needs to succeed and show what a good student he is, sitting down to do his homework when he said he would, even though he feels like doing something else.

Some children don't do their homework and don't have to pay a price: the teacher doesn't check, they manage to get it done at the last minute, or they find other solutions. It's none of your business. A child needs to get caught once without her homework done, and come and tell you about it without being told off by you. The price she pays can't be within your relationship but must be paid in the field of the real, at school. Every child wants to do well at school, just as every child wants to win when playing a game. They just don't fully understand yet what's required of them to be successful. And indeed, something different is required of each child. There is no one recipe that makes a good student. Every child has assets she can use and places where she will have to make an effort. But how will they know what's required of them if we take away the possibility of them managing themselves?

Sooner or later they all learn how to read and write. The more complex question is how to raise a child who knows and feels that he's smart, who doesn't give up even if things are hard, a child who expects success, takes responsibility, is pleased with himself, relies on external encouragement but also has confidence in himself. Take the pressure off the homework, don't organize their schoolbag for them but with them, and find in them all the qualities required of a good student: curiosity, resilience, responsibility, deferral of satisfaction, wisdom, creativity, the ability to ask for help, and the ability to concentrate. Pull your sleeves up and take a flashlight—you're heading out to find these qualities, and you will find them: some are out in the open, some are hidden, some are almost nonexistent. Now tell them every day, if they show even an ounce of such qualities, that that's called responsibility (he watched over his sister for three seconds); that's called being a child who doesn't give up (she rebuilt the Lego house that came apart); and that means being wise and curious and having the ability to concentrate (he solved a crossword puzzle with you, knew one word out of thirty but kept on trying).

The first natural thing we do when we lose control with them is try to regain the control. We tempt them with prizes, threaten with punishments, nag, or get angry—but these are the last things we should do with tasks we want them to own. When they're little it might still work, but when they hit adolescence it will turn into: "I'm not doing my homework—what are you going to do about it?"

Remember that in adolescence their life's mission changes. You and your contentment are no longer at the top of the list. Now what their friends say carries much more weight. Their head is spinning from dealing with the social field, their self-image, and other hard questions that flood them at unexpected moments—"Who am I? How do I look? How popular am I? Am I like everyone else? Am I special?" And just then, the hardest and most demanding part of school arrives, with subjects that they feel have nothing to do with their level of happiness, teachers who they feel don't understand them, and, above all, your disappointment, the pressure and criticism in the house—"She does help out," "She doesn't help out," and other complaints.

"Egotists" we call them, and we're actually a little right about that. That's what they are supposed to be to decipher who they are in this new adolescent format. It's exactly when they are this age that we have to realize that we can't force a child who doesn't want to learn. And if we hurt her, we are putting the only safety net there is during adolescence—maintaining a good relationship with her—in jeopardy. At this point we really do have to realize that all we can do is offer our help, private lessons if she likes, even reminders about upcoming exams, but this task is hers. And if she hears about the qualities that she does possess rather than about the ones she lacks—even if they have nothing to do with school but are about what she does at her other activities—she should be able to handle the task of school without paying too heavy a price.

The only tool we have to light their path is the simplest one of all: encouragement. If you don't get excited when he comes home with a D plus after getting a D on the previous exam, how will he find ways of encouraging himself? Children who are equipped with the knowledge that they are smart even if they didn't excel, diligent even if they did forget to get their homework done, and good students not because they got an A+ but because they finished doing their depressing homework and didn't quit in the middle—these are the children who will expect success and won't be crushed by failure.

— twenty-five —

No to Spoiling

WHEN THE TWELVE-YEAR-OLD BROKE HER CELLPHONE screen for the third time, I really had to restrain myself. The last time it happened, we agreed that she would use a special cover we got her, one that actually protects the device, but she naturally preferred a fashionable cover with glitter that better represented her personality these days. Her cries of horror rang through the house as if she had just lost her two parents. I ran into the kitchen thinking that something terrible had happened to her. When I realized it was only the cell, I switched to my parental role, which was focused mainly on stopping myself from slapping her or reminding her what we had agreed last time it had happened, on avoiding thinking about how much this was going to cost me, how I could get her to kiss my feet and tell me how right I was, how wrong she had been, and why next time she would have to listen to me and her father.

Soon enough her yelling stopped being directed at the universe in general and the god of cellphones specifically and began being aimed at me, for the simple reason that when I saw that she was unharmed, I left the kitchen without a word. "What sort of a mother sees her child in a state like this and doesn't help her?" she shouted at me. I replied that when she calmed down, we'd see what we could do. "What sort of a mother doesn't hug her child when she's crying like this?" she shouted, following me.

I looked at her, her face wet with tears, red and so angry, and again I had to resist. Resist telling her that she's not angry at me but angry at herself, but because she can't contain it she's taking it out on me. I also had to remind myself that this had nothing to do with me right now, that it was her and life, her and her responsibility, and this device, which symbolizes her independence in so many respects, now reflected in its shards the hardest thing of all, the thing you can't take back—one mistaken decision, one moment of carelessness. "You want a hug? Ask for a hug and I'll give you one happily," I said (even though I felt absolutely no happiness).

"Not like that!" she screamed, and slammed the bathroom door behind her.

I stayed in the living room, resisting for the third time.

After six long minutes in the bathroom screaming about how her life sucked and what a mother she had and wondering what she would do now, using "shit" and "fuck" and other words that should have provoked me to explain that this was no way for her to talk, that she had to calm down, that what needed to be done was A, B, and C, she stepped into the living room. "Mom, I've calmed down. This is what we'll do. I'll pay for fixing the new screen from my savings. I can take the phone to be repaired alone, but I'll be happy if you could help me. Until the phone is fixed, I'll call you from [her friend] Yahli's phone, because chances are we'll be together. And I'd like a hug, please."

Again I resisted. I stopped myself from asking what we'll do the next time, checking what she learned from this whole thing or how sorry she was on a scale of one to ten. Mainly, I resisted asking why she thought that the whole family deserved to tolerate her screaming. I hugged her tight and whispered, "Look how grown-up you've become. You're learning, solving problems. You're a star."

Our job is to not focus on ourselves, our egos, our worries, our insults, or even our clear educational agenda. Our job is to gradually let them get in touch with life, take responsibility, learn independence. When they are just twelve, we can fix their screen, but at twenty-seven we want them to fix by themselves everything that breaks, even their hearts. We want to know that they can cope with terrible things that might happen to them and, at the same time, to own wonderful things that occur. We want to teach them to count on themselves, on the powers they have, on the resilience they have developed and that we helped develop in them.

A three-year-old can walk around the playground alone, without you following her about. She can get dressed alone, soap herself, give her baby sister a pacifier, help prepare supper, offer solutions to your problems, sort socks, buckle herself in the car; she can cope with being unsuccessful at a game without you having to compensate her, let you take a nap, and fall asleep by herself at night. A three-year-old can do many more things that you had never imagined. It might take time, it might not happen in a day, and on the way she might get dirty, fail, make you prefer doing it yourself because it's more efficient or faster. But if you believe in her, she'll learn to believe in herself. Now imagine what a seven-year-old could do, never mind a seventeen-year-old.

So why do we do things for them? In the name of efficiency? Control? Lack of faith? Good parenting? Even if we raise children who hear plenty of praise, if they're not independent, they will never really feel their worth. Your words will be pleasant, but if your children don't encounter them in the realms of responsibility or independence, they will always feel inferior, victims of circumstance, angry, avoiding things, helpless. It's true that the world is sometimes a scary place, and going grocery shopping with a list when you're just nine and a half will take ages, the change might get lost on the way home, or you might end up forgetting the milk, but the feeling of an independent child who manages his own affairs, solves problems, is responsible for doing his homework or for not doing it, who really helps out around the house, at school, in society, who contributes and is significant, capable—there's nothing like that feeling in the whole world.

The spoiled child is the one who receives unnecessary services, who gets things done for him that he could do himself. And the job of doing is a hard job for a spoiled child. You are actually in charge of his life's reality: you dress him, bring him water when he's thirsty, carry his kindergarten bag or school bag, make and serve him his hot lunch, clear up after him, invite friends over for him, drive him to afternoon classes and wait outside for him, as he demands. You do homework with him, remind him about upcoming exams, improve his presentation, buy him something new every time something breaks or gets lost, call the kindergarten teacher, school teacher, or friend's mother every time something goes wrong, make the hard decisions for him, pay for what he needs and wants or wants and doesn't need. If you could only chew and swallow for him, you'd do it happily—all you can do to spare him sorrow or pain.

I'm not talking about random spoiling, making a cup of hot chocolate, helping them get dressed once in a while, or even making them an especially tasty sandwich or warming their socks in the oven before they put them on. I'm talking about pampering as the entrance ticket to life, about doing things for them even though it's perfectly clear whose job it's supposed to be. I'm talking about a child who believes that you're supposed to do things for her, that this is your job as a parent.

The spoiled child is one that hasn't got the emotional capability to do for herself. Someone invested a lot of energy in doing things for her, and by doing so has taken away her ability or willingness to believe in her own competence. The spoiled child is the one who will blame you when something goes wrong, even when she's twenty-seven. She'll get angry at you if she has to walk or make her own sandwich; won't help around the house because it's not her job; and when she fails an exam, in relationships with friends, at class, in relationships at work, she will never take responsibility—it will always be someone else's fault.

The spoiled child's parents are exhausted, often helpless, maybe mad, but mostly they feel as if they don't have a choice, that if they don't do it—no one will. In the beginning, when the child is younger, the spoiling parents feel like good and dedicated parents. All the unnecessary actions they perform for the children give them a sense of control, of positive pampering. It takes time for them to realize that they are actually damaging their children.

Quitting spoiling is a little like quitting drugs. You can't one-sidedly retreat from offering services, leaving the child without the tools to cope, or use words to explain to him the mistake and his magnificent potential abilities that will now have to come into play. The only possibility of quitting spoiling arises through your patience, through separating the process into baby steps that are accompanied by excitement, encouragement, appreciation, and awe. It's not the child's fault that you made the mistake of dressing him for seven years or begging him to do his homework. He isn't supposed to develop the life skills that a person usually accumulates over years overnight just because you decided that enough is enough.

A child who learns independence at a later stage needs the exact same things she would have needed if she was just four: she needs you to believe in her, to not give up, to not criticize or rush, to truly appreciate every advancement she makes, and, mainly, to trust her to make it through, even if she's angry or frustrated. She can handle it, and your job is to slowly remove the wheelchair you spent so much effort building, to see her take her first steps in the world of independence and just feel excited.

Sometimes, especially when they're young, it's hard for us to understand the part we are supposed to play in their movie. It's obvious that in our movie they have a lead role—after all, they are our children, they're ours! With them we became parents; with them we feel meaning, control, closeness, intimacy; in them we invest everything we've got and everything we haven't. You can't imagine the temporality of this story, can't imagine that something that is yours and that you love so much will one day leave you and set out on their own path.

During the first act, the rope is held pretty tight. The cord that connected us on the inside becomes external, emotional, and both sides hold on to it for dear life. But gradually, we have to let go of this rope, which tells the story of the relationship. And let's jump to the end of the script, just to calm ourselves: the rope is never fully released. It always connects us and them, and, even after we're gone, it will signify everything we are to them and they are to us. But here comes one of the hardest parenting tasks: to hold on to the rope here and now, and, at the same time, perform the distant, future mission of letting go. And what does that mean exactly? It means that even when they are just five, we have to ask ourselves what sort of adults we want them to be at twenty-five and gauge whether the paths we decide to take here and now serve this parental vision.

The quality of the rope itself and its strength depend on the relationship between us and our children's level of independence. The independence to solve problems and make choices and mistakes, to take responsibility, dream dreams, feel positive and negative emotions, be significant and contributing. The independence to leave the nest and build a new one.

To gradually develop that independence, we have to realize that the work starts the moment they are born. Every day we have to let the rope go a little further so that they need us a little less. And us? We'll always play supporting but very central roles in the story they tell themselves about themselves. It sounds very passive, but the action of releasing that rope—or resisting or not criticizing or not solving their problems—is very active. We will always be there on the other end of the rope, but when they fall into potholes, they'll have to climb out all by themselves.

twenty-six

Losing Control Doesn't Have to Be a Loss

SHE'S SITTING OPPOSITE ME, A FRIEND IN DISTRESS, speaking her pain in such a precise and conscious way. "I remember the first time I felt as if I didn't have enough air in the house," she sighs. "I was seventeen. I packed a small bag. I didn't have a plan, just the need to be in a place where I could breathe. She shouted at me that I wasn't going anywhere, called me 'young lady.' My legs took me to Yifat's house. There was plenty of air there. Her room was a mess and no one shouted at her because of it; she wore really cool clothes and nobody commented about it; Duran Duran's posters stared back at us from the walls and she put on a cassette of sad songs we had made together. We lay on her bed and I could breathe again."

She sighs again. "But you know what hurts the most now? The thing that hurts the most is that I've turned into a mother who takes up her little girl's air. It didn't happen with the boys. It's so easy with them. But she, she just wakes up in the morning and from the look in her eyes I know I've turned into my mother. I feel she hates me, that she feels just like I felt when I was seventeen, and she's only ten. Anything I say—she says the opposite; she disregards every feeling or need I have; every innocent conversation turns into a battle. Here we are, three women, three generations without air, and I feel like running away to Yifat's house again. The first time I ran because of my mom, and now I want to run because of my daughter."

They are born to us, they are ours. We are supposed to protect them, take care of them, teach them so many things, and, all this time, feel like we are in control. Because we are parents, because we read and watched experts explaining about boundaries and authority, because we were intimidated into believing that if we're not authoritative we will spoil them, that children need rules. So we try to be in control. It gives us a good feeling, introduces an inner order. When we're in control of what they eat, what they wear, how they behave, who they play with, which afternoon classes they go to, when they do their homework, and which content they consume, we feel like good parents. But there is one thing we don't take into account: our children are their own people. They are little people with a whole world of wants, experiences, interpretations, tendencies, loves, and preferences. A whole world separate from our own, which ticks in front of our eyes, proving every moment anew what a fragile thing control can be.

We need control in order to feel like good parents, and they need control in order to develop. And in a struggle for control there is only one winner, ladies and gentlemen, and it is always the child. It might take time, at the beginning you might feel as if you've won, but as they grow they will teach you a lesson about losing control. So you'd better ask yourself if it honestly matters who he plays with in the yard when he's seven or what she chooses to buy at the store. Ask yourself if it's really worth insisting on what she wears when she's four, if it's really that important that it looks right, if it really matters that it's summer and she wants to wear her sport shoes or put a costume on to go to kindergarten. Because to her it's not about the outfit right now, it's about her will. We say no so easily to the short dress and to so many other things she wants that it doesn't really matter what rational explanation we give—we are disregarding her right now, taking the control away from her; we're winning and she's losing. And then, when we hear her say, "You can't decide for me!" or "You won't listen to me!" we still don't stop to listen or to understand that this is how the oxygen in the room gets used up.

The foundations of the fourteen-year-old adolescent already exist in the six-year old, and she is offering a deal you can't refuse: "If you just respect me, who I am, my wants, my mistakes, my silly dreams, my choices, but really respect them, out of the understanding that you're raising a separate individual—then when you say no and it matters to you, when you say a no that's aimed at protecting me, I will be able to handle it. I will obey you without feeling as if you just passed a terrible verdict, which is exactly what you would want, right? You'd like to have authority in the places where it's really important to have it." But you don't gain authority through struggles for control, punishments, and sanctions. You gain authority through respect, good relationships, attentiveness, giving in, and saying plenty of yeses. And when you say the no, it's much clearer, and even if they aren't happy about it, they know that they have to respect your boundary, because you respect their boundaries, who they are.

This means that you'll have to give up on the feeling of "being in control," but I promise you, it isn't really a loss of control.

When they grow up you'll see that they absorbed the things that are really important, because when you try to control things that aren't that important, they automatically resist and argue about everything, fighting for their own breathing space and suffocating you. The end goal is not to resist saying no, because your face, sigh, tone, or whispering over their head will make it obvious that you don't approve. The real change will come when you realize that 50 percent of the things you insist upon should be released. Not because you'll lose, even though that's just not true, but because they, the kids, not you, really are the greatest experts when it comes to themselves.

Among my own children are those I find it easier to give in to because I see that their every choice does not oppose my inner logic or, worse yet, oppose me personally and in principle. These are also the children who, surprisingly or unsurprisingly, are more like me and remind me of myself. The demon of authority awakens with the kids who are different from me, the ones I worry for deep inside, asking myself: "Have I succeeded with them? Are they really growing up to be people who have the same values that I do?" With them, I have to remind myself, at least once a day, that letting go is not giving up authority but is respecting. Yes, also at the cost of their not living up to all my expectations. I always remember that even if I have lost some points in authority along the way, I earned the right to watch them grow by my side and I remain significant to them. And that's worth more to me than having the last word.

twenty-seven

Life with Screens

SEVENTEEN YEARS AGO, WHEN I GAVE BIRTH TO EYAL, we bought a camera, and once a week my father would pick up a little bag of used-up film canisters. The first grandchild taking his first bath—three rolls; the first grandchild seeing a dog in the playground—two rolls. Everything was documented and taken to be developed in the Kodak shop. The stimuli that Eyal was exposed to were our expressions, noises in the kitchen, guests who popped in from time to time, my incessant talking, a CD of children's songs, a picture book with over-bright colors, an old Winnie the Pooh video that I used as a babysitter when I wanted to take a shower.

Shira, my fifth child, came into the world to the sound of a carefully selected playlist from Yuval's phone played on a Bluetooth speaker in the delivery room. She had her picture taken even before the umbilical cord was cut, and her image was sent out via WhatsApp to her siblings and relatives. Her siblings prepared a "Welcome Shira" music video, which she had to watch when she was just one day old. Today, at the age of five, she is exposed to dozens of electronic sounds, inferior series on the Dis-

136

ney Channel, social networks ("Let's take a photo of Shira that makes rainbow colors spurt out of her mouth and turns her eyes into cat eyes"). In fact, she knows how to control every app that I, her father, and her siblings have on our phones and, most of all, she sees our eyes looking at the screen.

We can have a long argument about the price a child pays for spending their childhood in the shadow of screens, but one thing is perfectly clear—screens are not going anywhere. And although I have respect in my heart for all the educators and preachers, you won't hear any warnings from me or tips on how to leave the screens outside the home (even though it's an interesting experiment). As far as I'm concerned, screens are part of the world we brought them into. No one would dream of removing the fridge from their homes or managing without toilet paper on alternating days. Technology will always take something from us and give something in return. We, the parents, are charged with the job of supplementing the vitamins that the screens take from them. The sun is a wonderful thing, you can't imagine life without it, but when it's burning down on us we need to put on some sunscreen, sit in the shade, and even wear a big hat.

Before anything else, let's think about ourselves. The parent who used to hear messages on the answering machine or hold a book he was reading in his hand is now seen by his children doing one thing most of the day—looking at a screen. A child doesn't know that a lot of your screen time is spent working, answering emails, reading something that's work related, getting important info from an online group, and that only some of your time is spent playing addictive games or scrolling endless feeds. In the child's eyes, the parent is using the screen to do the same thing a child does with the screen—play, see something funny, amazing,

something to annihilate boredom. The stimuli screens offer people of all ages are powerful and riveting on levels that were never
experienced in our childhood, and they are always available. The
combination of our addiction to screens and having the option to
divert our children to a screen (instead of sending them out to
play with the next-door neighbor) when we want a bit of peace
and quiet is lethal.

And so, in the age of screens, we must evolve as parents and
take charge of human contact. We can't count on school, we have
to equip them with the knowledge that, despite all the wealth available online, there is no greater happiness than intimacy, attentiveness, laughing together, developing emotional capabilities. Their
success in this new world doesn't depend only on their grades or
their level of functioning; it also depends on their emotional intelligence, their ability to voice themselves, to listen to others, to
make human contact—and this is what we are responsible for.

Don't think that by not buying them a smartphone when they
turned nine you've solved the problem, and don't hide behind
limiting screen time and peeking into their phones, because that's
just telling yourself a nice story while they're burning in the sun.
You have to remember that pressing the picture of a cow and hearing it say "moo" is nice, but hearing Daddy say "moo" and then
laughing is an entirely different experience; eating in front of the
television may serve the concerned mother's aspiration to end the
evening and be sure her little one has eaten properly (when they
are young and their eyes are glued to the screen, the mouth opens
up automatically and you're free to fatten the goose), but there is
nothing like a twenty-minute supper where everyone sits around
the table, Mom tells everyone about something that happened at
work, Dad pulls a funny face, and when he gets a phone call he

says, "I'm sorry, I'm busy with a very important family dinner. I'll call you back later." And even if we don't manage to get a few bites of pasta, two pieces of cucumber, and some cheese and tuna into our four-year-old's mouth, we've achieved far more. Yes, we can let them fall asleep in front of the TV once in a while, but we have to remember that there's nothing like falling asleep after a story, a cuddle, and some loving words whispered in their ear.

Even as they grow up and, yes, enjoy watching TV or playing video games, they still need the simplest human interactions: to share a story from school, cook together in the kitchen, ask for your advice. Create tasks for them—helping you fold the laundry, doing Sudoku together, drawing a little picture together. The important thing is not how you choose to give them the vitamins, but the communication, the conversation, the touch, the intimacy that accompanies these vital nutrients, and no screen can compete with that. When you have fun together, look them in the eye, tickle them, watch a cat walking by and try to guess if it's sad or happy and why, and accumulate lots of other little moments like that during the day, you can live in peace with screens.

When they are adolescents, try to take a break and be there with them—to understand what that game is, how that app works, what his favorite series is. There is nothing like watching something together (topped with our annoying questions) to realize that we might not relate to the content they consume, but, after all, it's not that bad. Talking with an adolescent is the most important sunscreen of all—not a scolding conversation, or one whose aim is to get out some more information about his life, but a conversation that is really interested in him. Try to find one subject in the universe that you think your adolescent is interested in, and talk about it. Because letting her look at makeup and nail polish videos on YouTube all day long isn't like talking to her about it.

When a child is four you can still turn the computer off, take away the cell, and filter content, but when she's fourteen you'll be an ineffectual and insignificant element in her life. "The screens hijacked my adolescent" is what many parents say. But screens haven't taken her anywhere—she's right here. You just have to swap your toolbox and work differently, because she still needs you—for a good chat, for going out at night to get an ice cream together, for eye contact, touch (Yes, touch. How long has it been since you touched your teenager? Don't be bothered by their display of embarrassment when you hug them—they need touch just as much as you do), and anything else you choose to do together—if you can just put your phone down for a minute.

twenty-eight

Sharing and Sharing

B EFORE THE AGE OF CELLPHONES, WHEN I HAD TO WAIT in line to use the only payphone on the whole base during my army service, she would write to me. Our commander would appear with a pile of letters wrapped in a rubber band and read out the names. Not all the girls got letters, but I was lucky. Every evening a letter arrived from my mom, sweetening those hard days in which everything familiar was replaced by new smells and sounds, quite a few tears, and plenty of loneliness. They wrote separately. Dad would send funny letters, cut pictures out of the newspaper and add his own titles: a photograph of a house after a fire—"Life without you"; a photograph of a male model in a cigarette ad—"Remember what I look like?" My mother, on the other hand, would tell me in great detail what she did that day. I could imagine her sitting in the evening by the kitchen table, starting every letter with "Einati my Love." No one besides her called me Einati.

You can't imagine what that little *i* of endearment can do for you when you're alone on an army base. She told me what she had cooked for lunch, about her day at work, about how our cleaner was doing and the conversation she had had with her about the difficulties she was having with her children. She wrote about what she was feeling, whom she had spoken with on the phone, and sometimes she spiced it up with some neighborhood gossip—the daughter who was accepted to an exclusive course, a teacher who had left the school I went to. Once in a while she would stop writing to do something with my dad or Rani, and then tell me that she just got back to writing, leaving two empty lines to emphasize the pause.

There wasn't a lot of emotion in her letters, no expressions of how much she missed me or any existential thoughts. There was only her daily routine, documented with the boundless patience of a mother whose daughter had been drafted into the army, who knew exactly what she really needed. These precious envelopes that arrived every evening gave me my home, straight into my veins, the daily routine that continued while my world was turned upside down.

Think about it for a moment—whom do we share our daily routine with? Whom do we tell about our day at work? who we bumped into on the street today? how we waited in traffic? and other punchless stories? Whom do we tell about our thoughts, the dreams we dreamed last night, an annoying insect bite that's itching, or a pair of trousers we really like? The little stories of life, the ones that don't really convey anything, are dedicated to the first circle, magically knitting the closest relationships. The deep thoughts, the photos, the witticisms, the wishes—these all find their way onto our social network feeds, the more distant circles. Paradoxically, the connection to Wi-Fi brought with it a very concrete disconnection, which is especially palpable within the family unit.

And there's another thing. The children aren't given an equal status in this respect. We do our best to care for their every need, protect them from life, and carefully milk them for information about how their day went, who they played with, what they ate, what they learned, who offended them, but we neglect our part in the deal. What do your children actually know about you? What do they know about your fears, about how your day went, about how you fell in love or chose your job? What do they know about what annoys you (the things that aren't related to the mess you have to clean up after them every day)? When was the last time you told them some story without a moral about the rain that caught you on the way to the car from the office, about the cat with the kittens you saw beside the supermarket, about your worries, about the presentation you have to give at work tomorrow or the series you watched last night, falling asleep in the middle and having no idea now how it ended?

Telling our children things is an important daily mission. It's important because it gives the children perspective, allows them to practice listening, and helps them realize that we are also human beings. But it's especially important because it gives them the feeling that they are important, because it's only the most important people in the world whom we tell about the little things, only with the most important people we're brave enough to talk about our dreams, our mess-ups, the silly things that happened; they are the only ones we can tell about the lemon that fell off the tree and hit us in the head or the greengrocer who kept talking and talking when we were too embarrassed to tell him that we were in a hurry.

People like hearing pointless stories because it makes them feel significant, and when they feel that, lo and behold, suddenly they have a genuine desire to remember things that happened to them that day and share them with us. So don't pick out only the important points and talk about them alone with your children. Be sure to tell every child how your day went, share and share and share, because that's what makes our children empathetic, that's what emphasizes us being part of a human fabric. It connects us more than anything else and turns them into little people, short but so very important.

When I moved into my small apartment in Tel Aviv with Yuval, I threw out a lot of memories. The apartment was too small to contain all the pain and longings I dragged along from the life I had before our great love. I remember the moment I sat opposite the bathroom cupboard at my parents' house, took out the dusty shoebox that contained all the letters she had written to me, and threw it away. She wasn't around any longer to stop me from doing it. But if she had been, she would have probably said, "Einati, keep two or three of them." I miss her handwriting to this day, but her daily routine lives on inside me.

twenty-nine

How to Talk About Sexuality

S EX EDUCATION. WHAT IS IT BESIDES AN EMBARRASSING memory of a teacher in junior high standing in front of a sketch of the human body? Who even talked about things like that when we were children? And we turned out okay, didn't we? And what about our own ability to be open and talk among ourselves about sex, sexuality, pornography, urges, masturbation, and other topics? It would be much simpler if we didn't have to deal with it and if our children just understood these things as they developed and transformed into sexual beings.

Let's pause for a moment on this "we turned out okay" thing. In the past, this information was not so easily available. The worst that could happen was that a child, who still experienced herself as a child on almost all levels, would feel alarmed and shamed when she suddenly encountered something unexpected regarding sexuality. Today, on the other hand, we are dealing with an influx of information into the home that's only a click away, and that information reaches the children directly—unorganized, not necessarily backed by any educational agenda or even realistic or factual details. The child is forced to deal with information that she has no ability to interpret on the emotional level, and we fall asleep on our watch and wake up in alarm when our child uses her sexuality in places where she still can't deal with the consequences, when she has to cope with peer pressure and doesn't want to be perceived as weak and so goes along with it, when she joins the big leagues when she is still just a child.

The thing is that, to us, they always seem too young to talk to about sexuality. It's a story we tell ourselves so that we can take our time and go on speaking to them in the language of birds and bees, switching channels when a kiss appears on the screen, or telling the four-year-old that the tampons she saw in the bathroom are a special cleaning aid. The truth is that they are never too young. They have to get truthful answers to questions when they are very young so that when they approach adolescence they don't feel as if they should be ashamed or find out everything by themselves. You really don't want to leave this topic to the mercy of the internet or their friends' older siblings. You also can't plan that when they turn seventeen, you'll light a candle and sit them down for a talk in which the fathers explain to the boys and the mothers explain to the girls why and what they should be careful about. Because unlike the time when we were adolescents, they will already be past thousands of confusing sexual experiences of different kinds, and you will be embarrassing and irrelevant.

The foundations we lay when they are young leave the communication channels open for the days they really won't want to talk to us anymore. It's precisely when they are "too young" that they can get explanations about how children come into the world, what a menstrual cycle is, when and why people hug—it is just like explaining to them about the seasons, the neighbors' divorce, or where the milk comes from.

When they're young, they will ask innocent questions out of curiosity that will probably embarrass only us: How does the baby get into Mommy's tummy? Why are they kissing like that with their tongues? Why do you have hair down there? What's a pad? Why do you and Daddy lie naked in bed?

At first, they need to hear the basics and mainly to feel it's okay for them to ask and for you to answer any question. On one hand, you don't need to give them the full anatomy of everything—a sentence or two will do. On the other hand, you don't have to be afraid of saying that Daddy's penis goes into Mommy's vagina when they really love each other and really hug and really want to have a baby (and by the way, even when Mommy and Daddy don't want a baby, it's still really fun for them to do it in private and it's called making love). The baby is made out of a sperm that comes from Daddy and an egg that comes from Mommy. All the sperm join a race to reach Mommy's egg, and the best, smartest, funniest, and most talented sperm wins the race and connects with the egg.

Don't be afraid of telling them that you don't know something and will get back to them with an answer after you check or of asking them, "Why do you think that?" Try to sense when you've already answered their question and are just adding information that's no longer interesting to them. When they're older, ask whether it embarrasses them to talk about sex and tell them that you also feel a little embarrassed, but that it's nice to also be able to talk about things that embarrass you. Don't forget that they are asking out of pure curiosity and are not yet really touched by the subject, so most of the embarrassment is on your side.

Surprisingly, they catch on to cautions and warnings quickly. Whether, at a younger age, you talk about the ideas of "my body is my own," "private parts," "stranger danger," and so forth, or when they are adolescents, about condoms, sexually transmitted infections, unwanted pregnancy, and so on. You're actually less necessary there. We want to teach them to love their body, the whole of it, private parts included. We want them to know how to masturbate when the time comes, or at first just to know that it's fine to touch themselves, that it's a wonderful and pleasant thing to do, but it's something better done in private (just like you shower in private or go to the toilet in private). We have to teach our girls that women have a menstrual cycle each month, and you bleed and sometimes it is unpleasant, but it's a good kind of blood that reminds us that when we are grown-ups, thanks to this blood, we can have babies and become mommies. And no, children do not come by stork or jump out through your belly button; they come out of there, and so this blood is not like the bleeding you get from a cut, but a happy kind of blood. The same should be explained to boys about nocturnal emissions.

We want them to know that there is a chance that they will accidentally watch films on the internet and be very scared because they might see naked people there doing things they don't understand. So if they come across naked people while searching for "Anna and Elsa," they should tell you straightaway, and you promise to explain everything. The important thing is to talk with a language of love and geniality and use the future tense: "When you grow up and have a partner of your own, you'll also touch each other and it will be really fun (before, on the way, it will seem disgusting to you, which is also fine)." Be sure to give the feeling that "the door is always open" and have a conversation that registers as: it's fun to talk with my parents about everything; there is nothing that can embarrass them, worry them, and make me not ask questions, feel ashamed, or ask someone else.

Remember that we have given birth to a new generation of children and it will be hard for us to filter the content they are exposed to along the way to adulthood, so it's important to give weight to the moral places underlying sexuality. When they are adolescents, it's important to tell them that porn often distorts reality, takes the soul out of the whole thing, and leaves us with mechanics that might be arousing but that are very inaccurate. Tell them that sex shouldn't necessarily look or sound like that, and if they want to watch that's okay, but they need to remember that this is not what they should do when they have a partner, that the best part is finding out together what feels good.

It's important to tell them that most boys have performance anxiety and most girls have relationship anxiety, to explain that sexuality is something that does not happen all at once but gradually, and even to mention that when they and we both think they are ready to head out and play, they really may not be ready emotionally, and that's also fine—it happens to everyone. It's important to tell them that pleasure isn't guaranteed when you just get started, but if they listen to their own bodies and learn how to communicate with their partners, it will get better and better and be really enjoyable.

It's important to remind them that, just as there is peer pressure around alcohol and drugs, there can be peer pressure around sex. They should not kiss, make out, or have sex if they don't want to or just because someone pushed them into it. You can also talk about the fact that sometimes their sexual identity is very clear to them, and other times it is not, and that it's okay to be confused and to explore, to get scared and to check, but they should never forget that it's called "sexual identity" for a reason: it's part of who they are. Make sure there is an atmosphere of openness in your home so that all in the family can talk about things that are less pleasant and be present in their inner emotional picture. Present yourself as one whom it's nice to talk to, not only about successes but also about failures, not only about the things they know but also about the things they don't know.

thirty

The Social Minefield

S HE CAME BACK FROM BALLET CLASS ALONE, MANAGING to hold back the tears until she got almost home, then came inside and broke down. At first I couldn't understand what had happened. Her face was dusty from their activity and sweaty from the walk home, and unintelligible syllables tumbled out of her mouth. I gave her a glass of water and sat down opposite her, listening, letting her pain come out, without asking any questions. Again, she was insulted by the other girls; again, they didn't even notice she got insulted; again, she felt alone, tried to get over it, join in, be easygoing, hang in there. But nothing helped her to feel a part of the group. When they're in a group, they can be mean—she knows that from kindergarten, when she got the nickname Spit Girl, which one of her friends jokingly gave her and all the other kindergarten children quickly joined in on. She used to spit once in a while, a minor sensory regulation issue, almost unnoticeable, but kids see everything. So they saw and laughed, almost every day, and she survived it and became stronger. But now my brave girl was far from her stronger self, dealing with the most complex experience a person can deal with in the social sphere—the experience of rejection.

I'm raising a person who is different from me and it's really hard. She's stubborn and I'm not; I don't always know what I want but quickly recognize what others want and deliver the goods— she's the opposite; she stresses and I'm calm; she's a drama queen, erratic, quickly loses her temper, looks out for herself, gets easily offended, is self-centered, is an adolescent. And sometimes I panic and forget that under this display, which seems like my perfect opposite, there is a warm and large core of similarity.

I feel like I should take away her pain, tell her that they aren't worth it, call the mothers of the girls in class, those who are so sweet when they visit us at home but turn into a pack of predators when they're together; maybe I need to move her to a different school or find out what part she played in this story. When she was younger it was much clearer. I knew I wouldn't intervene, I would trust her, let her grow up and survive, and with a hug and a kiss it was over. But then my little one got bigger, the crying got less endearing, her hardship became more associated with our differences, and I didn't know if I could help her. And who would help me? Who would tell me that it would pass, that she'd get over it, that tomorrow she'd go to school and manage to cope with it? And who could guarantee that one day she would have one good friend? One, because you don't need much more. One was enough to not walk back home alone. Who could promise me that I taught her everything she needed to get along with the pack?

I listened to her story and put myself aside—the worry, the pity for her, the anger at myself, the sorrow about my acute failure in creating an easygoing child who wouldn't get offended too easily and who would know what it takes to be part of the group and deliver the goods. I put aside all my educational messages and realized that it's her story and it's hard enough for her as is. She was not looking to me for solutions; all the solutions I had in my mind were, after all, my own and for myself. So I suggested that she take a shower and that I would keep her company, and when she came out of the shower I wrapped her up in a white towel, just as I had done when she was still my little pup, kissed her, and she indulged me and hugged me. I whispered that she was wonderful and told her how much I loved her, that tomorrow was a new day. I asked her permission to brush her hair and told her how much I'd missed doing it. We remembered what silly hairdos she'd ask for when she was little, and laughed.

Sometimes, they gain understanding and learning even without us doling out any particular advice, setting a painful mirror in front of them, being disappointed in them, or judging them. It comes from a place of the so-challenging humility, from our ability to accept them the way they are and realize that they still haven't finished learning.

The things that children know about themselves, about their real characteristics, are what allow them to use these characteristics outside the house. So leave the "my little princess," "my gorgeous child," "you behaved so well today," and so forth for a moment. All that's great, but it doesn't actually tell them anything clear about themselves. Every time they exhibit a clear characteristic, name it and be impressed specifically by it, while they are exhibiting it, so that they can relate to it. "You know what you just did? You showed flexibility. You're a flexible child.

Flexibility is not only in your body, it's in your heart, too, and agreeing to play a game you didn't want to play with a friend, and even enjoying it, shows that you have that quality."

Remember the flashlight? Use it to search for the qualities that you think might be missing in them. You'll find them, because they are there—small, waiting for someone to shed some light on them. Tell them that they are generous, even if they're just sharing a snack; tell them they know how to get over things, even if they stopped crying only an hour later; tell them they're good friends after they barely manage to get a half-friend to come over and play; tell them that they're brave and know how to overcome their fears after they dare to ask the server for a glass of water.

They already know their stronger traits and will get to know them even better. You are the trainers of their self-image muscle, of whatever sits forever in the inner container of their soul. Remember that when you worry or get angry or disappointed, feeding them with sentences like "Why does it always have to end with an argument when you have a friend over?" or "Why do you have to be so stubborn?" all you're doing is taking from them, emptying their container. And then outside, in an increasingly challenging social sphere, they won't be able to cope on their own.

If I know that I'm smart, then when another child says "you dummy" I can get offended, but I'll know that it's not really true. If I know that I am loved, and I hold experiences and memories with my friends, siblings, and other children of my inner circle, then when someone isn't playing with me I won't feel as if the loneliness is something I created. Instead, I'll see it as a fleeting moment in a wider experience of social belonging. If I know that I'm a person who can come up with creative solutions, then when something goes wrong and I feel I don't know what to do,

I'll remember that it's actually no sweat for me to find a solution. If I know that I'm a girl who knows what she wants (stubborn) but also knows how to be flexible when necessary, then when I come across an impossible social reality and nothing works out the way I wanted, I know I have a choice. I don't have to freak out, and if I choose to, I know that at any moment I can try something else.

We are not exposed to their social sphere—we only get reports about it. We're the first aid that waits for them outside. They come out to us wounded and bruised, after paying a price for their own mistakes or others' mistakes, which we have no control over. The paramedic's job is to bandage, put some ointment on, treat the pain, and trust them and life so that the next time they go out there, they won't fall, or if they do, it will hurt less or they'll try something else.

thirty-one

Don't Break Your Heart

WHEN WE HAVE A CHILD, A LITTLE ROOM OPENS IN our heart with his name on it. In this room lie our deepest wishes for him, and at the top of the list is that his heart won't get broken; that he doesn't experience loneliness, shame, bitter failure, hardships; that he won't get offended; that he'll have an easy path and be happy with his lot, because happiness widens the heart. The problem is that every time this child copes with a breakup or hardship, something in our heart also breaks a little. And when our hearts are broken, we are no longer at our best, we are no longer sharp enough to produce what our child needs from us.

When they're really young, our hearts can break when an older child takes their place in the line to the slide. We see our little baby's face looking up at the child who just walked past him, encountering injustice for the first time, realizing that he's small and so can do nothing, and only his chin trembles. Later, the harder experiences come along: "No one played with me at recess." "I studied so hard but still failed the exam." "He broke up with me in a text message." "They didn't let me join in." "I got stood up." How many times have you felt like driving over to the house of the child who insulted your son or told your daughter that she was fat and ugly, or to the school to find the teacher who asked him to stand up in front of the whole class and show everyone whether he had done his homework, to knock on their door and explain what terrible, flawed behavior they brought into your space? Because whoever hurts our child has to answer to us and our broken heart.

We mistakenly believe that the fact that our heart breaks puts us in a more caring, more empathetic position. We think that if our heart breaks for them it makes us slightly better parents, because what kind of a parent can stand back and see his child in pain? But, in fact, when our heart breaks they know it, and their room in our heart stops being a safe place for them. A parent's broken heart, even if that parent doesn't say a word, is one of the heaviest burdens a child can experience.

Try to imagine meeting with a close friend, the kind of get-together we arrange to unburden ourselves. Imagine yourself voicing your pain, sharing something and crying, and then the person sitting opposite you also breaks down. She breaks down because your story reminds her of herself, because it touches a soft spot, because in your story her own pain also dwells. Now the roles have changed. There is no longer a person helping and a person getting help, only two broken people. Imagine yourself sharing the same story with a therapist, in the safety of the clinic, and the therapist taking a tissue because he can't hide the emotional overflow he's experiencing.

If our heart breaks, it is always at the expense of the one seeking our help. It's true, we're also human, but we have to realize that it burdens them, that it has no value, that we can't really allow ourselves to be the wounded ones while their hearts are bleeding. And we have to have a serious talk with ourselves about it, because a child who gets pitied learns to pity himself, and a child who breaks our heart will think twice about whether she should tell us of her troubles.

On the other hand, a boy who gets offended can identify when he's being hurt, a girl who gets her heart broken is a girl who knows how to love, a sensitive child is also sensitive toward others. We need to look for all the reasons in the world not to break, to look at their hardship with an empathetic smile that clarifies that we totally understand the ditch they've fallen into—the pain or insult or shame—but we're not really worried. Our job is to offer the point of view that knows they're only going through a rough patch, developing well, experiencing hardships that we have all experienced. True, it's not easy, but we're here to tell them that it only feels like it's the end of the world. When they climb out of the ditch—and we have no doubt that they will—they will feel differently, and the other feelings, the good experiences that await them, will heal this wound. And when another wound comes along, another ditch they'll need to climb out of, we'll always be there for them.

In my heart there are five rooms with children's names—a room for Eyal, Yoav, Lihi, Rona, and Shira. At the entrance there is also a room with Yuval's name, because this heart was his first. My heart is full of scars, wrinkles, and pains that all, without exception, have made me the person I am. All the failures, hurts, and losses allow me to be happier, stronger, to look at this hard life with gratitude and reverence.

And of course I sometimes ask myself what life would look like if my mother was still alive, if Yuval's sister was still with us, if the twins we lost were part of the family, if the difficult challenges each of our children faces would just disappear. Who would I be then? What would my days look like? But then I think about the last ex who broke my heart before I met Yuval and thank him for calling off the wedding; remember that I went to study my favorite profession after crashing and realizing that being a lawyer was not for me; think of the years it took me to manage to bring live children into the world and the kind of mother I am to them because of this hardship. I remember those who are gone, whose acutely marked absence is the imperative of happiness in my life.

It's clear to me that my children's hardships are indirectly mine, too, but I don't confuse my job of coping with their individual processes of coping. My heart guards their rooms in it, so it cannot break. And I wish them hardships alongside happiness, failures alongside successes, edifying scars, reinforcing pains, and I won't allow my heart to break for them, not even for one minute.

thirty-two

How to Protect Them from Bad Friends

OUR KIDS FIRST VENTURE INTO THE SOCIAL SPHERE when they are still very young, equipped with the private logic imprinted in them at home. This logic is destined to encounter hundreds of private logics born in other houses, completely different ones, and this process of socializing is exciting, enthralling, painful, pleasant, and, most of all, unavoidable. This is one of the most complex tasks of life they will encounter.

In this social forest there is beauty and shade, there are predators, and there is a sense of freedom; there are sweet fruits and poisonous mushrooms, and our children will have to experience this forest and learn. The social learning process is gradual and has plenty of nuances, which is why they will get through it—the forest will not get the better of them. Our job is to narrate the movie for them, translate the interactions they have there into emotional language. For example: "It's very unpleasant when another child tells you to do something you don't want to do. On one hand, you don't want to say no, and on the other hand, your heart tells you it's something you don't really want to do. So what should you do?"

When another child is hurtful toward them and we prohibit them from interacting with this child ("That's it—you're not seeing him anymore") or offer advice that doesn't necessarily fit our child's personality ("Tell her you're not playing with her anymore"), we leave them in the forest without a water supply. In this gap between our wise advice and the child's personality in life in the forest, many mistaken conclusions can arise, such as "If Mom and Dad think this child is so bad for me, but it's so much fun for me to play with him when he's not hurting me, I just won't tell them that I do play with him or that he bothers me, so they won't be disappointed."

Often we also come along with future insights—they're still in kindergarten, but we're already thinking about their married life. They still have a long way to go, and they can't read our guide to surviving life in the forest to help them gain the ability to distinguish friendships that benefit them from friendships that are pleasant but also unpleasant and friendships that completely take over and are really unpleasant. They need to constantly experience the forest and learn. The account we offer as narrators can't be too anxious or overprotective and also can't dismiss them as small people. The narration has to explain the situations they encounter as they are and accompany them through the process of learning.

Don't distance another child just because you don't like her. Instead, be grateful for the fact that your own child has encountered this child and can learn things about herself through the other.

The accumulated experiences of dealing with the girl who bossed everyone around, the one who was nice only when we were alone and turned her back on me when the others arrived, the one who always had a good word for me but whom I mostly ignored, and the bitchy one who always snubbed me but whom I still wanted to hang around—all these experiences were necessary stops on the way to my own future wedding.

The moment you lay aside your apocalyptic visions, you can narrate your child's movie better, understand the complexity instead of trying to blur it. You can encourage your children when they recognize situations that aren't right for them or courageously dare to speak their mind or even show flexibility for someone else's benefit. This helps them view you as a nonjudgmental entity and share complex experiences with you, knowing you can accept their hidden wish to be best friends with the rowdiest kid in class (because they're a bit geeky) or be the queen of the class's second (because they aren't really cut out for the job of queen) or fight with someone weaker (to feel stronger themselves). It's best to experience these and many other experiences over and over again so that they get to know themselves better and can move confidently through the social field, the forest.

What we can do is encourage reciprocal relationships. And here's a charming and naive theory that's worth keeping in mind: if, in a relationship, each side is in charge of the welfare of the other party involved, instead of his own welfare, and both parties are equally responsible for the happiness of their counterpart, the magical equation of relationships would be solved. And so, every time your children find themselves in relationships that give them respect, that don't pose impossible terms, that allow them to be at their best on one hand, and are there for them when they really aren't at their best on the other, explain that the reason why they feel good is not because they don't fight at all with that friend or because they are very alike—it's because the contract of mutual respect and equality they are enjoying is making them good friends in that relationship.

When it comes from a place of encouragement, they are willing to listen. So instead of: "Of course he offended you. Wait, it's just the beginning. You only learn the hard way," try to find the places where what you see is to your liking, and reinforce these places: "It's amazing that you have a friend who is willing to give in and to stick around when you're sad. That's what's called being a good friend" or "I really respect you for telling your friend you don't want to throw stones with him, even though you felt as if you might want to. It means you feel secure enough with him to say no." These are moments you can use to explain what the really important things are. And no, the idea isn't to sit them down for a talk—these things should be said as part of daily conversations; sharing our own social experiences with them or encouraging them indirectly in a way that helps us illuminate the places where they recognized the right thing to think or do, even in the most unpleasant social interactions (and yes, you will have to overlook the eighty other mistakes they made at the same time).

In the list of important things, these are the points you might want to emphasize:

~ Friends who constantly criticize you are not worthy of you. Don't find yourself in a relationship that includes mostly criticism. It accumulates and becomes unpleasant.

~ If you're friends with someone and everyone around you is wondering about it, not only your parents but other friends too, think hard—it just might be that everyone is right.

~ If you're interested in being friends with someone who is far less interested in being your friend, see it as a warning sign.

~ If your friend is nice to you when you're alone but changes her behavior when other children are around, it can be very confusing and insulting. Ask yourself what it is that makes her change her behavior and see if this way of behaving allows you to go on feeling close to her.

~ Sometimes, the fear of being alone (especially in adolescence) may lead you to choose company that isn't worthy of you. We won't intervene or make choices for you, but beware of situations that keep you in a relationship that takes much more than it gives. Any relationship in which you are constantly inferior isn't worth having just to avoid loneliness. Also, it keeps you from finding new, exciting, and interesting relationships that could take you to new places.

~ It takes time. Even if we, your parents, tell you that we met at fourteen, it doesn't mean that necessarily has to be your experience.

~ You can enjoy different types of friendships—have one friend you go out with, another you can call when you're down, a third you can study with for exams. You can find the right things for you in each of your friendships, the things that you'd never agree to let others say to you and the things that you can live with, even if you would prefer them to be different.

thirty-three

Bullying Is the Limit

A T NOON, BEFORE THE GREATEST HUMILIATION OF MY life, I stepped onto the school bus. A thirteen-year-old child in an innocent yellow bus filled with children of all ages. The destination: home, back from school. The object: surviving the journey. Surviving Shahaf, the school bus bully. I had to get through this journey twice a day, each day, back and forth. No matter which seat I chose, he always found his way there, not doing much, but still managing to intimidate me. He would sit behind me and blow in my ear. Sit beside me, snatch my schoolbag, and start tossing it back and forth to his friends. They were really tall, Shahaf and his eighth-grader friends, always in a good mood, laughing, once in a while whispering my name from the back of the bus, like something from a horror movie. And I would just lower my eyes, stare at the floor of the bus. My body knew just how long the ride would take. I was the first to get off when the doors opened, and I always had a bag full of soap with me that I'd prepare at home. When my hands were busy playing with the bag, I had something to focus on and the fear was more tolerable.

That day, I got off the bus and walked home through the basketball court. I heard them behind me, him and his amused friends. I remember the soap bag in my right hand, the hand squeezing too hard, and the bag suddenly tearing, the soapy liquid spilling on the court and on my trousers. Within seconds, they surrounded me, as if I was a birthday girl celebrating the end of the age of innocence, there on the basketball court. Shahaf came up close to me and whispered: "I'm willing to overlook the fact that you just peed yourself, but I won't ignore the fact that you peed on our basketball court. So you be here tomorrow morning with a bucket and mop and you clean this basketball court. Clean it well so that I can forget this unfortunate thing ever happened, got it?" I got it alright.

Next morning, I woke up very early. Dad and Mom were still sleeping when I took the bucket and mop from the balcony. I filled the bucket with warm water, which made me think of a nice, warm bath, and I left for the basketball court. I finished mopping pretty quickly, leaving some puddles of water on purpose so that they knew I had kept my end of the deal. I got back home before everyone woke up, put the bucket and mop back in their place, and got back into bed, waiting for Mom to wake me up, trying hard to pretend that this morning was just like any other.

One of the prayers that should join the list of parental prayers—among the ones for health, finding a place in the social sphere, finding true love, and many other prayers we dedicate to our children—is, "Please, God, make sure my child doesn't suffer from bullying." If we use the forest image from the previous chapter, the real danger is not a deep swamp or stinging nettles, not even dangerous animals, but that moment when a tiger approaches with its mouth wide open. At that moment, it is our duty to guard our kids and point out the danger ahead.

Kids constantly encounter bullying in the social sphere, but there is a significant difference between randomly meeting a bully in the schoolyard and regularly encountering a bully who becomes a threatening shadow that has found a particular victim and bullies them daily. Such behavior doesn't have to be especially severe. When examined individually, each encounter may seem like a normative part of managing life at school: a little slap on the back of your neck; a leg that trips you on the way down the stairs; a sharpener that disappears from your pencil case and is suddenly thrown around from hand to hand; an insulting nickname that touches a nerve; a "funny" noise hummed every time you walk into the class; blocking the entrance to the restrooms; even just passively following you down the hallways.

Your child, who hasn't come across this kind of unrelenting bullying before, will try to survive in the shadow of the other child, who finds it amusing and fun to perform these ongoing acts of bullying. He won't always be able to tell you and will often take the blame himself, feel ashamed, or worry about how you will react. He might often refuse to go to kindergarten or school. If you watch him as he walks there in the morning, you might notice he's walking differently, faster at times, sadder perhaps, and his gaze will be a focused look instead of a peripheral one, as if scared to encounter it—his daily nightmare.

This type of daily, cumulative, humiliating bullying that repeatedly comes from one source—no one should deal with it alone. Not even an adult. This kind of bullying signals an existential threat, and we need to get our child out of the situation, just like we would jump into the deep end to save her if she hasn't yet learned how to swim. The wonderful advice that served us and her in coping with random acts of bullying—go to the teacher, talk back, ignore it, turn your back on her—won't work against a bully who has targeted your child, and often makes things worse, because the bully isn't going anywhere, and the victim, she just wants to disappear, to stop being. So, yes, unlike many other situations where you're better off staying out of it, here you should release the protective lioness within, become the helicopter, enter that sphere and remove the obstacle.

Random bullying, the kind almost every child experiences at one point or another, can be discussed with children, because it's a good idea to equip them with tools that will help them understand how to cope. Here are some truths they should know about bullying and about themselves before they encounter it face-to-face:

~ The bully, to be a bully, needs a victim. If you aren't a victim, he can't go on being a bully. What does it mean, not being a victim? You can smile at him when he insults you, you can ignore him, you can call a friend over and talk with him about a series you started watching yesterday. You can hum a song to yourself, maybe ask the bully how he's doing today in response to anything he says or does. There are endless creative solutions you could come up with (and it's also worth asking the children—help them distance themselves from the situation, to imagine it happening to another child, and to think what advice they would offer that other kid).

~ It's important to remember that a child who bullies is often unlucky, because someone in her life must be treating her badly, and to ease the pain, without being aware of it, she is acting in the same way. Often we mistakenly believe that a bully's behavior is a sign of strength, but it's important that our children realize that it's actually a sign of great weakness.

~ We often hear the expression "words can kill" in the context of bullying on social media. It's important to remember that words only have the power that we give them, and we cannot give power to the words of a bully. You can tell your children to talk to themselves while it's happening and remember that these are just words.

~ Being nice to a bully sounds like a crazy idea, but the truth is that the best story we can tell our kids is how a guy stopped next to us at the traffic light and said some very unpleasant things, waving his hands and even scaring us a little, and we decided to open our window and answer him. "And you know what we said? We said 'Have a wonderful day!'"

thirty-four

Talking About the Wolves

M Y BELOVED GIRL, WE'VE BEEN RAISING YOU FOR NINE years now, seeing the good in you so that you learn to see it in yourself; accepting your mistakes with forgiveness and understanding so that you know that even when you feel you're not delivering the goods, the greatest pleasure is to improve, learn, reach conclusions. We taught you how to be polite by being polite to you; taught you how to treat others kindly by letting you see us smile upon the weak, be forgiving toward aggression, interpret others' actions favorably even if their way is different from ours.

Nine years have passed since you were born, and we can see that when we are clear about our limit, you always live up to our expectations, understanding where someone else ends and you begin, recognizing your own boundaries, saying when something is pleasant and when something isn't; arguing when needed, going along with things when required, and, mainly, identifying injustice or wrongdoing and saying it out loud. And I feel that now, even though you're just nine, I have to talk with you about men and women, about things you hear in the news, about a topic that is confusing and unclear, even to us adults—its title is "harassment."

The title "harassment" brings us to complicated tasks of life, such as building self-esteem, establishing boundaries, finding your inner truth, and, most of all, encountering wolves. Yes, just like the wolf in Little Red Riding Hood, the one she was warned about. He, in his cunning, dressed up as Grandma, pretending to be someone else so that he could devour her. I told my girl that in places like these you have to be very alert, very connected to yourself, to what's good in the world and, also, to what's bad in it.

Why am I talking to you about harassment even though you're only nine? Well, the truth is that there isn't an age when you can't or shouldn't discuss unpleasant things, and it's more a matter of my readiness as a mother to talk with you about things that aren't easy to talk about. Your father and I will always think you're too young, we'll always feel the need to protect you and give you the feeling that the world is a good and safe place. This is why this conversation is hard for us, and it doesn't really matter if we have it when you're nine, six, or thirteen. The important thing is that this conversation serves as an unburdening encounter with complicated information. Don't worry, I know that as the years go by we'll be able to talk about it from different perspectives, and that I just need to highlight this conversation as important so that you'll ask when needed later on. As you grow and the more we talk about it, you will gradually realize how important it is and how helpful my words could be.

I know that you already know how to identify wolves. When you were younger we explained that there are people who are sick with a disease that isn't visible on the outside, a sickness of their heart and their soul, and they could sometimes try to do things that cause you to run away or immediately call the adult in charge. We already told you that if anyone offers you a ride from school, you should not get into the car. We have explained that your body is your own, and you were taught the same important lesson in kindergarten—that no one is allowed to touch your body. We might have confused you a little when we told you to give Grandpa a kiss even though you didn't want to, even adding, "Look how sad Grandpa is because you won't sit in his lap." We might have made a bit of a mistake there, we should have given you the feeling that you really know best where you end and someone else begins, when you want to do something and when you don't, even with close people, even with Dad.

And now you sometimes watch the news with us and hear talk around us, and it's probably the right time to talk about the wolves that disguise themselves, making them harder to recognize. I'm talking with you about it so that you know that we can talk about everything in our house, because when you don't talk about a certain topic, it can sometimes be interpreted as shame, and when you're ashamed of something it's usually because you're thinking "something's wrong with me" or that it is not okay to talk about certain things. As a result, when certain things happen, we keep them to ourselves instead of telling someone about them. So remember that once in a while we'll talk to you about things that are a little embarrassing, and remember that it's also a little embarrassing for us, but we're doing our best to teach you everything we can, so we must talk to you about wolves in disguise.

It Has Nothing to Do with You

First of all, you should know that it never has anything to do with Little Red Riding Hood's red dress. Never think that the way you look, the way you behave, your confidence, your short dress, or even the openness you project are any reason for someone near or far, teacher or instructor, acquaintance or boss (when you're older) to see you as something to touch, hug, or sleep with (when you're older). It's not your fault if you find yourself in a situation where someone offers you an indecent proposal like "Let's hold hands" or "Why don't you come over and sit in my lap" or "Let me stroke your hair" or "Let me touch your body." If you remember that it has nothing to do with you, that it only has to do with the other person and the way they are interpreting the situation, it will be easier for you to understand that there is nothing to be ashamed of and that nothing you did or said gives anyone the right to do to you something that you're not interested in having done.

It Sometimes Takes Time to Understand What's Going On

There's a good reason why Little Red Riding Hood asks Grandma so many questions: "Why are your eyes so big?" "Why are your ears so big?" and so on. Sometimes, especially when it's someone close to us, it takes a while to realize they're a wolf and not a granny in pajamas lying in bed. It takes a lot of courage to say "something isn't right here." At first you'll have to say it to yourself, and then the fear will usually talk back: "And what if I say no and he gets angry?" "What if I cry 'Wolf' and it turns out this person actually isn't a wolf?" "He said that if I told anyone, I would miss out on a high grade" or "Maybe it's all in my head and I just have to go along with it? Because Mom and Dad always say that sometimes you have to do things that are less fun in order to succeed." This is the point at which you have to overcome your pounding heart, the fear, and the confusion and realize that there is no price too high to pay for the freedom to decide for yourself. Sometimes you'll realize this after you've already made the mistake or allowed someone to do something that feels wrong—remember that that's also fine, that it's never too late to recognize your own boundaries, redefine something you defined the wrong way. It's never too late to ask for advice or tell me or Dad.

You Have to Be Brave

Things that feel wrong sometimes require brave and extreme action on your part. Just as we taught you when you were still in kindergarten—if anyone says or does anything unpleasant, even if it's your friend, you have to say, "Enough! Stop it! I don't like this." And as you learned yourself, if that doesn't help, you can always tell us or the kindergarten or school teacher. Here, too, you need a lot of courage to tell someone bigger or stronger than you: "Enough! Stop it! It's not okay!" And sometimes the other person will stop but it will still feel strange or uncomfortable and you'll have to tell a friend or me or a grown-up you trust, because when you talk things over, you can think together about the best way of dealing with a wolf. Sometimes, you might pay the price of shame or breaking a promise, but you'll just have to realize that you are doing the right thing.

Wolves Are Weak

Even though it might seem to you as if this person could devour you, that they are bigger and stronger than you, you have to remember that a strong person doesn't have to use force, promises, or sharp teeth to make you love them, do something with them, kiss or touch them. A really strong person asks you, asks for your permission, checks whether it's okay for you; strong people won't have to disguise themselves as Grandma or threaten you not to tell anyone. And this is the wolf's weakness.

My love, remember how much you know, remember that even when life creates impossible situations, there is always an option, the choice is always yours. Remember that sometimes your body knows better than your head that being afraid of wolves is normal but giving in to wolves is not an option. Don't let a wolf cloud your confidence in yourself and in the wonderful world we live in, a world of good people, justice, morals, boundaries, and mutual respect. Take a deep breath, go visit your sick grandma, and put your goodies in the basket. Recognizing wolves, dealing with them, and warning others about them are for the brave, and you, my child, are a brave one.

thirty-five

Raising Boys Who
Won't Sexually Harass

W HEN WE BECOME PARENTS, WE HAVE ALL SORTS OF
educational hopes and wishes. It's clear to us that we want
to raise moral children who have self-confidence, who can tell
the difference between right and wrong, who know how to handle frustrations and hardships, who are wary of people who may
harm them but who are also trusting and believe in relationships.
We explain and mediate almost every topic, but somehow the
subjects of sexuality, couples, intimate relationships, and wooing
aren't taught at home. After all, it doesn't come naturally to talk
to our children about these things, and our parents didn't exactly
elaborate on these topics when we were children. To be honest,
just imagining such a conversation is enough to send shivers of
dread down our spine. And so, we send our kids out into the
world with warnings about perverts, at best, and hope that they
turn out to be good people and treat their potential partners
accordingly.

God help a parent who doesn't have an educational agenda
when it comes to mutual respect between the sexes. When chil-

dren grow up and enter the fray of intimate relationships, they often come across conflicting interests and contradicting signals: I want to and she doesn't; she wants to talk and I want to touch; she indicated something, but I misunderstood it; she wants to take it to the next step, but I'm not ready. And all this is mixed up with hormonal urges that rise up in the way of reason. Besides the image of a couple's relationship that they witness at home, we also have to equip them with our set of beliefs to make sure these values are entrenched deep inside them and that our children come to us in times of need. If we muster the courage to talk about it, they just might turn to us when something goes wrong. Every parent, according to their beliefs, style, and level of openness, is obliged to speak with their children about their worldview and positions on important topics.

So when he's three years old and he's playing with his little sister in the bath, we'll teach him to ask whether it's okay or if it's nice for her when he explores with tickling hands; and when she's four and the quickest thing to do is pull her clothes on or off, we'll ask her if we can take her shirt off or if she wants to do it herself, if the kiss or the hug feels pleasant or if she'd rather we stopped. And when they're seven, we'll talk to them about how babies come into the world, we'll mention the love, the pleasant sensation, and the willingness of both parties involved. And when they are twelve and watching the news with us, we'll say a few words about the sexual harassment incident reported, not necessarily saying how awful and terrible it is, but how confusing it can get and how you should never be confused and that it's always better to ask than to assume something is okay with the other person. And when we ask them about girls or about boys, we won't only ask what she looks like, what sort of a student he is, and what her last name is but also will ask what her expression tells him, if he knows how to listen to her when she talks, and we'll explain how important attentiveness is in a couple's relationship: listening to both verbal and nonverbal messages, looks, emotions, wants.

So, dearest boys, I know that you're still young and your hearts haven't yet felt the special kind of beating reserved for true love. However, your bodies and hormones are totally set on confusing you, so watch out and know that you will sometimes come across situations when it is not clear what's allowed and what isn't, what will serve you and what will cause trouble.

The wonderful new sense of sexual arousal that has taken its place in your body could find its way to magical, delightful places but could also lead you to the darkness of shame. I know you've already heard me say these things when you were very young, but it just might be that other parents haven't sounded these important messages to their adolescents, and it might help them realize that it is no less important than teaching politeness, road safety, financial planning, or how to be helpful to others. So here it goes.

You Also Want a Relationship

Girls use sexuality to achieve and enjoy relationships; boys use relationships to get sex.

Unfortunately, this is the reality you will encounter out there as an adolescent: the boys will talk about how far each one got and the girls will whisper to each other about the chances of mutually falling in love. But it doesn't have to be like that. The outer appearance or sexual communication you receive from girls could turn out to be a mutual interest in sexual contact, just as it could be an invitation to start a relationship. Don't be one of those guys who flaunts his number of experiences or which girls he's had or who joins in on discussions about the one who puts out and the one who isn't worth the time. Think where you would like to be on that scale, because you also want a relationship. When you're in a relationship with love and reciprocity, friendship and fun, care and mutual giving, I promise you the sex will be a thousand times better than casual sex with a girl who wasn't necessarily interested in it, who might not necessarily be happy after it. It's better to just masturbate or at least to talk about it with your potential partner so you know for sure that the two of you have similar expectations.

Have Sex Only When You're Willing and Ready

It takes time, practice, and, at first, there's no guarantee it will even be that much fun. Don't get into it just because the guys are bragging, because you think it should be over and done with, or because you're stressed that it might be time. Sometimes the guys' "talk" is nothing but talk, and sometimes you're just imagining that everyone apart from you is already doing it. Believe me, you've got so many years ahead to enjoy sex—don't rush into it. Make out, kiss, touch each other, hold hands—it's all connected. And when you meet a real woman and are really attentive to her, you'll see she will totally appreciate all the stuff around sex that you're now practicing. It's called romance and it's a big turn-on for women.

No Surprises

Unless it's in a jewelry box or is a bouquet of flowers—don't surprise her. Always ask. Worst case, she says no. A much worse scenario is starting to kiss her only to be pushed away. Just as I taught you to knock on the door before you step into someone's house, don't dare to barge into a woman's body. You might have seen it in films, one of your friends might have told you it was super cool when he just put his hand there or suddenly kissed her, but it is not cool. Even before you held hands with a girl for the first time, you asked permission, and if you didn't explicitly ask, your finger fluttered close to her finger, which agreed, and then suddenly all the other fingers consensually joined together. Consent is the key!

Each Side Is in Charge of Only the Other One's Pleasure
You're in charge of her pleasure and she's in charge of yours. Absolute mutuality. That is how the concept "making love" really materializes. Because in a world where everyone takes care of their own needs first, there is no room for true reciprocity, empathy, and trust. Generally speaking, if every person used his own choices and abilities to enrich the lives of the significant people in his life, and, at the same time, a significant other enriched and contributed to him, the world would be a better place. So when you're kissing her, open your eyes once in a while to see whether she's enjoying it; and when you want to try something new, ask her first if it's okay; and when her mouth or body say no, it's just not worth it, because having a momentary sense of pleasure isn't worth the feeling that you've just trampled all over someone. Even if she isn't crying or pushing, it doesn't mean she hasn't been trampled on.

thirty-six

Where Has My Little One Gone?

UNTIL RECENTLY, SHE STILL ASKED ME, "MOM, CAN I have a chocolate pudding?" "Mom, can I go over to a friend's?" "Mom, can I stay up late tonight?" Until recently, I could say no, explain why not, and contain her frustration or just make a silly joke. There were better days, worse days, but it depended mainly on me—the level of my attentiveness and patience. And when there were bad days, I could blame myself with painful honesty, promise myself that tomorrow I'd be more in control. How simple it was when they were younger. How simple it was when they were still shorter than me.

Sometimes I think it all changes when they grow taller than you. They don't ask, "Mom, can I?" any longer, just open the fridge, meet up with a friend, stay up late. When exactly did I sign a lease with these housemates, and why do I now have to leave a note on the last chocolate pudding in the fridge saying, "Hands off, you have a baby sister and this is hers. If you've reached this one, it means that you've probably already had yours. Mom." These days, it's not only about me, and even at night, after a tough day, I find it hard to reach conclusions for the next day. Instead, my heart beats fiercely because I just had a fight with a semi-grown-up to whom I gave birth, and he has a mouth that speaks harsh words, and I was offended by him and forgot he's just a kid. A fifteen-year-old kid, but still a kid.

It was so easy to forgive him when he was five, and now it is so difficult. When the sun rises tomorrow, I'll have to turn a new page. And he won't wake up wearing the cute pajamas I put on him after his bath; he'll wake up in his underwear after deciding not to take a shower last night, and he won't give me that four-year-old's beaming morning smile, the smile that made the whole universe smile, but instead will growl at me, the clock, school, life. And I won't put a bandage on his cut or keep the secret of what he's most afraid of; when he laughs out loud, it'll be with his friends, not with me; he won't follow me around the house; when I try to hug him, he won't fall into my arms; and he won't ask "Mom, are you cross?" anymore.

Parenting adolescents is a complex task. After finally deciphering the operating system of the child at a tender age and gaining experience in parenting, understanding a thing or two—suddenly, the operating system changes, and instead of updating to the new version, we lag behind, still responding in babyish talk even though our children are now speaking a different language with us, with themselves, with the world.

Adolescence brings along a separate life mission. If you manage to update your version, manage to fully understand it, you'll remain significant to them. If you don't understand it, you'll find yourself constantly battling in a losing war that is meant to reinstate your control and significance. In this war everyone gets hurt. It happens because you won't read the map correctly and because they are supposed to rebel, turn their backs on you and face their friends, find and reinvent themselves as an autonomous and independent extension, and feel that there is someone in this world who understands them and the neurological and hormonal craziness called adolescence.

So take a deep breath and realize that, from their point of view, you're still significant, it's just that your significance has taken a different shape. You don't feel it in the same way, and they certainly won't bother to fuel you with a sense of importance, because they're busy with their own task. One of the most important parental tasks here is not to get confused, even though the spectacle they put on is very confusing: they look and talk like adults, but they're still kids. All that remains to do is to hang in there and not give up.

And by "not giving up," I mean you should not give in when it comes to school, being rude, or leaving their shoes in the living room. I mean you should insist on giving them the feeling that they are important to you and find various creative ways of staying important to them. Because when she was three and threw herself onto the floor in a tantrum, you might have understood it's a developmental phase, realized that her behavior wasn't against you; you could hug or pity, forgive her when she calmed down, and offer encouragement. But when she does the exact same thing at fifteen, minus the floor and the tears, and with a ruthlessness and hatred in her eyes, it's a little more complicated to understand. And then, without thinking it through, you react sternly or meanly, because you get hurt. You're so worried that you've raised a wild child, that you feel an urgent need to set her straight instead of setting yourself straight before you react.

We're really not supposed to give them everything they want, but we *are* supposed to recognize the fact that the place that reacts inside us is the alarmed place of losing significance:

"You won't talk to me that way": insult, loss of significance; "You won't do whatever you want": control, loss of significance; "If this is how you behave, there will be consequences": revenge, loss of significance.

When you are dealing with an angry adolescent, remember that she is supposed to be angry right now. It's really okay. It doesn't mean you've failed in your parenting or that she's discarding you. All you need to do is look into her eyes, take a deep breath, and remind her how much you adore her, understand that she's pissed off, even agree with some of her arguments (even though they were not said very politely), and admit you're aware of the fact that parents are annoying when you're an adolescent.

If you don't panic, then they'll panic less (even though they won't be less angry. After all, that's their job in adolescence). Remind him and yourself that tomorrow is another day, and when tomorrow comes, go after him and clarify that he's essential to this house. Knock on the door of his room and find out how things are going, how school went; cook food that he likes to eat, don't give up on him at the dinner table, ask his opinion in a political argument, tell him about something that happened at work. They need us much more than they can or are willing to imagine. They need us to see that it's hard and burdening, that we see them with kind eyes, show interest in them, ask for their advice, share with them, laugh with them, argue with them about why school is necessary, tell them about our childhood and adolescence experiences, and tell them secrets we ask them to keep.

And then you'll discover that the whole story of significance at this age is a story of hard work, hard but rewarding. Because she might not wake up cute, snuggly, and adorable in the morning, but she wakes up and needs you just as much as she used to, and you need her too. And that is probably enough significance to get you through another day.

thirty-seven

When They Turn into
Our Messy Drawer

I've got a messy drawer in the kitchen, and I bet
you do too. Every time I open it, I look at the flyers, elec-
tricity bills, safety pins, sunglasses, cute but useless little tin
boxes, medicines that must have cured something before they
expired, chargers for devices that have passed away, batteries,
sore throat sweets glued to the bottom of the drawer, birthday
greetings, old pictures, invitations to long-past weddings, and
much other evidence of my dysfunctionality as an adult in the
private sphere.

The kitchen drawer is not alone. It's closely related to the
bags in the storage room and a whole side of the children's closet.
Yes, I'm Einat and I can live in a world that contains drawers like
these. You can simply close them as is, wipe the kitchen counter,
wash some dishes, and feel just fine about it.

There's just one little thing that bothers me. Every time I
open the drawer, or add another bag with goggles and a pool
towel to storage, I feel my parents' eyes looking at me. My mother's eyes say, "How many times have you said that you'd get this

mess under control? How come everything is so perfect on the outside and so messy underneath the surface? It's too bad that you don't invest a quarter of what you invest in your appearance in your room, school, or helping around the house." I hear her in my head and become the sweet at the bottom of the drawer, glued there among a collection of papers and unnecessary screws, seeing Dad and Mom looking at me with disappointment in their eyes.

Through all these years of meeting parents, children, adolescents, and families in the clinic, I collected many moving images of relationships. Of them all, the conflicts with the adolescent girl or boy are the most complex, despairing, and challenging. Find me the parent who says: "My adolescent? Totally fulfilling herself. Honestly—no complaints: she helps around the house, her room is spotless, she has a high grade point average; she is a Scouts' instructor, surfs, plays the guitar, and is a real social butterfly. She's interested in current affairs, keeps a high level of hygiene, and has high self-esteem. She doesn't lock herself up in her room, makes wonderful conversation, is exceedingly polite, and changes her sheets once a week." To this parent I would say: "Congratulations, you have an alien. You can join the Guinness Book of World Records." For most parents, the painful part is looking at them, our children, at that critical stage and seeing them as our messy kitchen drawer. We think that if we only criticize them enough, comment enough, argue, punish, and educate enough, our messy drawer will sort itself out and everything will be okay.

They ruin the fine order we worked on for so many years, and we don't understand what we need to do to make them take responsibility, learn, help, or consider the most basic things we brought them up to care about. We don't understand what went wrong along the way and how it turned out that every day we have to remind them to schedule a private math lesson, move their bag from the entry door, put their clean laundry back in the bureau, tidy up their room, hang the towel back in its place, call Grandma to say happy birthday, sit for half a second with their younger sister—do one thing, five minutes a day, that doesn't tap in directly to their pleasure center, just because it needs to be done.

We end up turning, like our parents before us, into people who can only see everything that isn't working. We see them as our messy drawer. We tidy after them, scold, complain, and never miss an opportunity to turn the whole thing into something personal: "Tell me, do you think I'm having fun every day at work? that I feel like coming home and cleaning up after you? that I enjoy seeing you in that same position of doing nothing and more nothing? What are we going to do with you? Why do you think that I have to do things for you when I feel that you're not making the slightest effort for this household?"

For the adolescents, on the other hand, it's a totally different experience. Right after they perfect the ability to filter us out as if we were nothing but background noise—and believe me, it's no small achievement, because we are relentless—they feel like our messy drawer. If we just allow ourselves to shut that drawer for a while, live with it as is, and tidy around it, we might be able someday to open it together and slowly, very slowly, sort things out, organize, throw out some old flyers, and smile at the sweet still glued to the bottom.

thirty-eight

Woo Them

THEY ARE THE COOLEST COUPLE I KNOW, AND I MEAN that as the greatest compliment. They totally nailed it. They have great jobs and are really fit. Their tattooed bodies, which once went out clubbing, now jog through the park, and the trips to Thailand have been replaced with an apartment in Berlin. They like to be generous, they're never short of money, and they own a house in a good neighborhood in the center of town. They ride bicycles and write short posts accompanied by amazing pics of restaurants, beaches, cocktails, and three photogenic kids. They talk about the right streaming series and the right books, drink the right wine and drive the right car, constantly maintaining a balance between modesty and an inner certainty that they are very cool. Until one day they found out that they had fallen asleep on duty, and that it's really, really not cool.

It started with a text that appeared one morning on the mom's phone. A parent of one of the fifteen-year-old kids found out that the children were getting drunk at parties, smoking, and riding in cars with older kids who had just got their licenses. The girls, so the message said, joined in with random acts of oral sex, which, after a sufficient amount of alcohol, took place "voluntarily." There were plenty of other awful and disturbing details that forced the mom to read and reread the message, while thinking that it must be some terrible mistake, an April Fool's joke, some sort of prank. Every possibility rushed through her mind, because there was no way this message could be talking about her child. She tried to think about the parties he had gone to in the past month. There were a lot; they didn't have curfews in their house, and that's what it's like being a teenager—summer vacation, you go out, party, come back at five a.m., wake up at noon. When he woke up, she always asked, "What was the party like? Fun?" just as she had asked him when she'd picked him up from kindergarten, and the answer was always yes.

She didn't respond immediately, as everyone else in the group did, but dialed her husband's number. He was in the middle of a meeting but always picked up, even if he was busy. She didn't call often in the middle of the day, and she realized from his "hi" that he was busy, so she just said she was sending him a text she had received and that he should call her back when he was free. He got back to her right away.

That evening, at the end of their workday, the cool couple met at home. They talked and realized that they had to invest some energy, that they had a job to do, that being the "cool parent" isn't always cool, and that there are some problems that can't be solved with just one talk or Google search. There are some problems that require a long and hard educational process, and sometimes it is the opposite of every cool instinct, but it is just what's needed.

They realized that even though their son looked like an adult, talked back like an adult, and dressed like an adult, he was still a kid. The assumption that guides many of us is "We were once adolescents too, and we got through it okay." After all, our parents didn't know what we got up to when we went out clubbing, who we went with, and when we came back. Now let's think about it again, this time through the parents' eyes. Yes, we turned out okay; fact is, we're alive, functioning, working, married. But are we willing to let our own fifteen-year-old participate in the experiment that's taking place today? Because it's a little different from what it was like when we were adolescents. The messages our children are exposed to today, every day, are violent, sexual, confusing, and disorganized. If the parental task used to be bringing information into the home, today the task is to filter out information and, mostly, to mediate which information gets in.

Imagine your children playing in a world of virtual reality on all the online games available, with all the props and the mental state of "being the game, not playing the game." Cool, right? Now imagine your teenager being exposed to porn (it happens for the first time when they are around thirteen or fifteen, not necessarily in your own house, but you haven't installed parental control on their friends' phones). When they are exposed to porn for the first time, they don't only watch it, they participate in it. Virtual reality, remember? So these kids set out into the world after having experienced a full sexual experience in the comfort of your air-conditioned house (as far as they are concerned), alongside various forms of violence, driving all sorts of vehicles, setting out on killing expeditions, playing in front of large crowds in noisy stadiums, and much more. The next thing that happens is that the adolescent's operating system—their emotional, cognitive, and physiological system—gets a few bugs:

1. They feel it's really cool to take risks.
2. They feel as if they're really grown-up and competent.
3. Everything you represent has little interest to them.
4. They want more and more independence.

As mentioned, the most important mission at this point of the relationship is to understand how you remain significant in a teenager's life. In order for your opinion, words, selves to carry any weight, you have to maintain a good relationship with them.

The meaning of a good relationship in adolescence is not drinking beer together. It is a courtship in which you are the ones wooing and they are the ones being wooed. You'll have to find good things to tell them about who they are, how they look, how much you enjoy talking to them. Every minute they dedicate to you is a precious moment in which you can establish a good relationship, ask for their advice, share things with them, show interest in them, truly listen to them. Invite them to keep you company while you're preparing dinner, take the opportunity of being in the car together to hear about their day, watch the news together, knock on their door and sneak in a tasty sandwich, hug them for a split second when there are no friends around, know the places where they are invested, respect them, and, most of all, root for them.

If there's any chance that they'll listen to you, that your opinions will live within them, that you'll manage to instill in them brakes that can contradict their developmental phase, it's only if you maintain a good relationship with them. If you are present in their lives despite the aloof spectacle they put on, if you allow them to share with you without jumping in with criticisms, if you are happy with them despite the tremendous challenge of parenting them—only then will you earn the right to forbid things, stop them, protect them even when they push back and reject.

When they were younger, you could tell them to stay in their room until they calmed down, take away their screen time, even take away things that mattered to them. An adolescent with whom you try to use power actually has more power than you have. When she runs out of the house and doesn't answer your calls, she'll prove to you once again that the most important thing from the very start is maintaining a good relationship.

And make a note to self: she will lie. There will be a point at which she will lie, not because she's a pathological liar, and not because you are bad parents, but because she has to. She is on a journey to define her separate identity, but she has internalized all your educational concepts, what you think or allow, and especially what you consider unacceptable, and she doesn't want to let you down, so she lies. You might not remember it, but you lied too when you were that age.

The most challenging parental task is to maintain an intimate channel for communication. A channel that allows them to tell us about mistakes, that doesn't set standards or expectations that they could never meet; a channel that will help us parents know what's really going on in their lives: when they are in danger and need us to jump to the rescue, when they're just wrong and need some good advice, and when they screw up big time and we need to think together what to do to make sure it doesn't happen again. We shouldn't do this because we don't tell lies in our house or because their lying really offended us, and not even because we'll never be able to trust them again—but because we really want to have a discussion that will clarify what their needs are, what the thing is that is important to us that they can't do, and where we are willing to cut corners for them, even if we don't like it, just because they are important to us. This discussion is not about lying or trusting, it's about the journey they are making, the mistakes, the lessons they learn by themselves, and the ones it's important to us that they learn.

Remember how, when they were younger, we'd say, "If only they would come to us when anything happens, so we can help them"? Stop being too critical and judgmental, stop focusing on yourself and on how offended you got, on your anger, on hurting them as much as you're hurting. Be worthy of being the first people they call when something really goes wrong.

It's actually their lying that can give you your best chance. They're lost, they screwed up, they were tempted and participated in the gang's alcohol and sex party. And then the lie oozes out, because they're really scared they'll disappoint you or make you angry, worried you'll punish them and say harsh words. This might be the opportunity to show them the way home, because they really do get lost sometimes, because at this age it's easy to do. Take advantage of this low point to surprise them. Turn the light on in the lighthouse and remind them where home is, where you always take them at their word, and if they lied, then it must be something very important to them that might be worth talking about. Even if we don't agree with everything they say, we can at least let a conversation take place, really listen to them, show our vulnerable side, tell them what we're really worried or scared about for them. What if we take advantage of that moment in which they're expecting a mouthful to do something coura-geous, the opposite of what we'd usually do? There is nothing that brings people closer together than vulnerability. There is noth-ing that builds more trust than a parent who won't give up on trust, even when the adolescent supposedly makes every possible mistake. There is nothing that brings you closer together than compassion, attentiveness, forgiveness. It's the most wonderful opportunity to bring the child back home, instead of scaring him off to the most confusing places waiting out there.

Sometimes we tell ourselves stories and cut too much slack. Sometimes we're not fighting over our relationship with them but are battling against them instead. Sometimes we fall asleep on duty. We have to stay alert and be present but also attentive and flexible enough to tell them what we think about drugs, al-cohol, and sex not only as part of a parental talk but also in the course of day-to-day life. Yes, sometimes we also have to limit their partying and make agreements that will respect both their needs and ours, and then face their discontent and protests with plenty of respect and love but without getting confused or letting anger or fear control us.

Take a piece of paper, think about your teenager, and make a list of all the dreams you have for him: all the qualities you wish he had, all the things you think he needs to improve in his appearance, his conduct, the way he talks and behaves. Now take your list, put it deep inside a drawer and open it up again when he's thirty. I promise you that if you focus on maintaining a good relationship, when you open the list together with him, you'll realize that it has nothing to do with who he actually is and what he turned out to be and has everything to do with the dreams and worries you used to have.

thirty-nine

Girl-Woman in Front of the Mirror

SHE STOOD IN FRONT OF THE CUPBOARD, A GIRL-WOMAN who, only five years ago, was laughing and spinning in a dress I had bought her, the dress whirling around her happily, as if celebrating with her. Now she was crying. I went into her room and found her standing in her underwear, the clothes she had tried on and hated scattered on the floor. We had to leave for a family event. I looked at the body that had come out of mine in what felt like just a moment ago. A perfect girl. The little tummy that bothered her so much would disappear very soon when her breasts grew; the wild and youthful hair; the smooth and fair complexion; the sad, despairing eyes. Even the tears that rolled out of them seemed young and fresh to me.

I thought about my own body, which had its history. The breasts that had breastfed five children; the wrinkles of laughter and crying that mark my face; the left hand that has become more muscular from carrying infants, and the right hand that learned to function alone; the small hunch that was the result of tiredness and picking toys off the floor; the womb that carried twelve pregnancies, of which only five were successful; the bags of sleeplessness and worry under my eyes; the crooked tooth I learned to live with; the hair that has grown thinner with births and lice combs. At that moment, I and my historic body faced her fresh body and broken spirit, and all I wanted to do was one of two things: take away her pain and help her feel more grateful or, alternatively, give her a good slap and make her stop behaving as if she was possessed.

One of the most present and unspoken conflicts between us and the young people who grow up in our house and who are called "adolescents" is the psychological complex that stems from the loss of our own youth and the defying presence of theirs. The man will get to see his strapping young son, the mother will see her daughter developing and turning into a beautiful young woman; and vice versa, the father will see his daughter developing into a sexual creature under his own roof, and the mother will watch her son growing up, knowing that in a moment he will give his heart to another woman. Consciously or subconsciously, we as parents will encounter all the things we used to be and no longer are.

Once, when adolescents reached puberty, they would leave the nest with a bag on their backs, marry, start a family or just leave for the jungle and, at best, drop by to say "hi" after their coming-of-age voyage was over. Today, the storm of adolescence takes place right in front of us, in our homes, with our money, over years and years. And we, who used to think that raising young children was hard and exhausting, face their spectacle of adolescence with a fair degree of pressure, shame, and good intentions, but no road map.

Our dialogue with our own body image is cruelly reflected back at us moms through our teenage girls. The culture in which we raise them doesn't make this easier and complicates the messages. But the story is ultimately a simple one: every parent's hope is to raise a child who loves her body, comes to terms with it, and enjoys the reflection staring back at her from the mirror, even if it isn't perfect in her own eyes or in the eyes of a culture that sanctifies slimness, prettiness, and beautification. But for a girl to reach this constructive place, she has to overcome complex hurdles that are far from easy.

Until recently, our little girl looked in the mirror with a nonjudgmental, uncritical gaze. Ours was very much the same. We took photos of her at every opportunity, asked "Who's my beautiful little girl?" We bought her costumes that, with a little imagination and secret wishing, turned her into a real princess. The gaze directed at the mirror was brief and unfocused, allowed her to sail away on the wings of fantasy, dance barefoot in the kitchen while her wand or twirling skirt did its job. But now that her body is changing, and with it patterns of behavior and thought, we compliment less, take fewer pictures, get confused by her obsessive preoccupation with her body, become alarmed and think that we have raised a superficial and egocentric creature who's in love with herself, sticking her tongue out for every selfie.

She, for her part, is beginning to be aware of the scary changes that are twisting her body's shape day by day, hour by hour. For a short moment, she looks in the mirror and manages to hold on to the image of "Mommy's beautiful little girl," but the next moment—on a bad hair day, when a zit suddenly appears, when her tummy sticks out a little more than yesterday, or when the clothes we bought her with hard-earned money suddenly look silly and ugly to her—she faces a black mirror that can show her nothing but despair and frustration.

Our job is to realize that having the fantasy shattered is inescapable—their bodies are changing almost every day and their mood almost every minute, and they have to vent their frustration. We need to remember how many years it took us to get used to our bodies, to learn what fits us and what doesn't, what puts us in a good mood and what's really hard, to internalize and recall that this voyage to womanhood is composed of so many compromises and acceptances but also so many strengths and victories. If we do that, we might also realize that this mission is far too hard for a thirteen-year-old girl. We'll realize that this is a mission that has to take place in stages and will sometimes bring a fair share of grief. And we, as our little duckling's parents, have to accept these complex stages on her way to becoming a swan in her own eyes.

Wanting to take away their pain or disappointment attests, among other things, to how difficult it is for us to bear the frustration we feel when they aren't content with what they have. So we set out to battle, armed with sentences that can't take away her pain: "What are you talking about? You're so beautiful!" "Are you kidding me? We went shopping only last week and you chose all these clothes yourself!" "Try on the denim skirt. You'll see how good it will look." "Easy—we'll go on a diet! That's what I suggested yesterday after you ate those three doughnuts." And there are also the old sentences from when she was three: "When you calm down, we'll talk about it." "Here we go again—I'm going to be late for our family event just because you're having another fit." "Just finish getting dressed without looking in the mirror, and let's get going," etc. If we put our frustration aside, our hidden criticism about her style of clothing, our inability to understand what it was that lit the fire of rage, we can walk her hand in hand through the moments in which nothing works out. We are the sponge that's supposed to take everything in, observe, accept what she's going through with an expression that shows her that it's really hard but that it's part of a process and that it will get better very soon.

On a day-to-day basis, while she's pleased with herself and we think there's no need to praise the cruel mix of trends she's selected, or just while exchanging a couple of words with her in the kitchen, we have to take a minute to give her a compliment, as specific as possible, one that could also serve her in front of the mirror: "Your eyelashes are the most beautiful thing in the world." "Your legs look great in short skirts." "Your hair looks so pretty tied up like that." "You look so beautiful in red." And when she uploads a photo to Instagram (and you feel sick at the sight of it), ask her what she likes in herself in this picture—the angle? the hair? the pose? Join her in places where she thinks she has a comparative advantage. And finally, if there's a little sister around and "Who's Mommy's beautiful little girl?" is still heard around the house, direct the sentence at her once in a while in remembrance of the days in which she still believed you.

I sat down on the floor of her room. She was red-eyed, defeated, hurting, and I, with a comforting and slightly pitying look, listened to the remainder of frustration and nodded, without saying a word, just being there, consoling the bereaved. When she took a deep breath and calmed down, I took her hand and stood in front of the mirror with her. She was only sniffling now. I stroked her perfect hair and looked at my own imperfection. I started making really ugly faces, and she couldn't stop herself from laughing and said, "Stop it, Mom." And then I whispered in her ear, "These days can be such a bummer, right? Do you want to pick out something from my closet?" When she chose the gray-white sweater, and after threatening her that if she stained it, it would be the end of her, I took us back to the mirror so she could look at herself again, and I said: "You're my star. Look how you got over it, look how beautiful you are." And for a moment, just a moment, she could see it.

forty

A Letter from an Imaginary Teenage Girl

Mom, Dad, it's me.

I know that it's strange that I'm leaving you a letter, it's just that with everything going on around the house lately, the words never come out right. You're really busy, I know, and you're mad at me and disappointed in me most of the time (that's how it feels, at least). I'm not actually that available myself (friends, moods, hours in front of the wardrobe and mirror, fights with my siblings). So I'm writing.

Even though you think I'm not listening to anything that we talk about, I wanted you to know how important you are to me and explain why it's so hard for me to deal with the way I look. You see, I look strange to myself. Sometimes, I wake up in the morning and my nose looks big, sometimes I have a disgusting zit and I'm sure that's the only thing people can see when they look at me. When I have a bad hair day I go crazy. I'm too fat. I'm in love with myself and then I hate myself—and all minutes apart.

I remember you used to think I was pretty. When I was little, Dad would always say "my pretty one." You took pictures of me all the time, the clothes you bought me looked really cute on me, and Mom always loved it when my hair was tied up. Now, I suddenly feel as if you're always disappointed by the way I look. And you know what's funny? Now, of all times, when I really hate the way I look, when everything that looks amazing on Noa, the perfect girl from class, looks stupid and awkward on me (never mind bathing suits), this is when I need you most to think that I'm pretty. I need you, Mom, to tell me you see me even when my hair isn't tied up the way you like. I need you to realize that, just once in a while, when I feel really pretty, and I'm standing in front of the mirror, the last thing I need is your "constructive" criticism.

It may seem superficial to you, the amount of time and energy I spend on my appearance, but it affects everything. On a day when I feel good about myself, I'm also a better student, a better friend, a better daughter, a better sister. It gets everywhere, this inner hatred. So when I'm finally pleased with myself and you make a comment, think about the fact that you just sent a less good student out into the world, a less patient person who is less able to deal with everything out there.

My self-image isn't stable or coherent right now and it's really confusing. Sometimes I'm down and other times I'm up, and sometimes I'm in a new place I barely know, the real pits, and then I feel as if I might never be able to leave the house again. And then you're there with the criticism or the disappointed expression, and I react as if you had just stepped on my broken foot. And you ask, "Why are you reacting like that? Can't I say anything anymore? What was so terrible about what I said?"

So listen, even though you assume that you're really not important to me, the truth is that you're in my heart, my stomach, my head. One good word from you can pick me up, and one word of criticism reminds me of the black raven who's sitting on my shoulder most of the time anyhow. And the worst thing is when you ignore me. Say nothing. One look from you, Dad, or you, Mom, is enough to lift me up or bring me down. Give me one compliment, clear, precise, that I can relate to. I know that you think that I don't like it when you compliment me, sometimes I even pull a face and say "Stop it," but what I actually want to say is, "Could you say something more?"

I want to love myself and it doesn't matter what I wear or what I did with my hair. I want to love myself and it doesn't matter how I chew gum or if I've gained a bit of weight lately.

Please remember: less criticism. And if you really have to criticize me and can't help it, just know that

even though you loaded me with compliments when
I was little, it still doesn't mean that my tank is full.
The memory of you being proud of me and of the way
I looked when I was younger is just more piercing on
the backdrop of the looks you give me now.

It's easiest to give compliments or offer a good word
to those who look perfect, but those who really need
compliments are the ones who don't look perfect.
I'm not asking you to be phony, I don't want you to
tell me how much you love me either (or maybe I
do), but I need to know through you what is beautiful
about me, inside and out, even if it seems to you as if
I'm not relating to what you're saying; all your voices
accumulate in the end, and right now most of them are
corrective, displeased, critical, and disappointed.

You always tell me that no matter what, I can
always tell you everything, and I ask myself—can I?
Sometimes I don't because I don't want to burden you.
I hear you talking late at night and don't understand
why my experiences worry you so much, and when
you really worry, I get stressed. Sometimes, I don't
say anything because I know you'll just dismiss what
I feel ("Fat? What are you talking about?" "You hate
your breasts? What nonsense!" "They didn't invite you
to the party? Their loss!"). Or just start one of your
educational speeches.

So understand—I do understand. Everything you
put inside me when I was a child is still there, I'm
just confused, and that's why I confuse you too.

Take a breath so that you can give me room to make mistakes, fall over, get back up, crash, love and hate myself, knowing the whole time that you see the better version of me, see me the way I should actually see myself in order to get through life. Okay?

forty-one

Their Fat Is Also Theirs

WHEN THE WEIGHT WATCHERS INSTRUCTOR EXplained to the adolescents in the room how to order a hamburger in a restaurant, I saw something break inside him. Her intonation changed as she listed the elements of the mission: one—no ketchup or mayonnaise; two—skip the top part of the hamburger—yes, you can enjoy a hamburger without the top of the bun; three—say bye to the fries, which, my friends, you already know about from our previous session.

I sat behind him and saw his back shift in discomfort. I saw how with one sentence, uttered with didactic sweetness and courteous assertiveness, the joy of his life had been eliminated. His liberty to see a hamburger as a holistic entity was shattered, and, most of all, the thing that was destroyed was the illusion he had managed to maintain for sixteen and a half years: he's actually fine, not someone who belongs in a club of people who sit in a group, take their shoes off, get on the scales, and share what temptation they had resisted that week.

This meeting was defined at home as a trial meeting. Before it came a harsh visit to a clothing store followed by a conversation in which he asked us, his parents, to help him lose weight. To be honest, I was happy about the conversation, not because I suffer from being the mother of a child who wears XL but because he initiated the conversation and wanted it. Years ago, I promised myself I would not join the forces that would make him feel damaged: the children who called him "fatty" on the playground when he was four; the voices in his head that sometimes tell him he doesn't fit in; the teacher in elementary school who made a snide comment; or the aunt he barely knows who joked about his healthy appetite on Passover Eve. I knew for sure that if I imposed the change on him without him completely understanding its deeper meaning, we might become the proud parents of a boy who wears M, but he wouldn't really be doing it for himself. He would feel like a hamburger without the top bun, without the ketchup and mayonnaise, and without his best friend. Yes, yes—the fries.

So when he asked for our help, I was moved. Talking with him, I realized that he had closely encountered what you gain and what you lose and was now ready and willing to make a change. I realized I was going to find him the right framework for this change, not because I wanted a healthier or more beautiful or attractive boy but because I wanted to open a window into the eternal dialogue between him and his food, the love–hate relationship there, the feelings of comfort and the feelings of guilt that follow. A window onto his body image, his masculinity, loving himself as is, experiencing success, experiencing resistance, experiencing real fullness and real hunger, the reason why he eats, and the reasons why he will eat differently. And this window will be his own private window, and the more he understands himself, the happier and more complete he might feel. Or not.

When a baby is born, one of the body systems that work perfectly is the one of hunger and fullness. The instructions are very simple: you're hungry—scream and food comes; you're full—close your mouth, turn your head away, and there will be no more food. In early infancy, there is profound meaning to the crying that demands food: you signal the need and the universe responds to it. How reassuring; how much communication in such a basic interaction. I search for the car keys, ask the universe, and find them; I want to seal an important deal, so I send a message to the universe and it's done. The confidence gained is double-fold: confidence in myself, in being able to say when I'm hungry, knowing my body and recognizing it is hungry; and confidence in knowing that when I tell my mother I'm hungry, she will satisfy this hunger, because she understands me, because I can count on her, because she is the universe and together we form a whole that I still can't form alone.

So every time we push a teaspoon into our infant's mouth when he isn't paying attention or give him a bottle just because it's time and not because he asked for it, or even when we pride ourselves on how he finished eating up all the fruit puree, ignoring the fact that he had closed his mouth and turned his head half a jar earlier, we have to realize that we're infringing on his secret contract with the universe, disrupting a system that's working perfectly well, and taking away the confidence he was born with.

And the situation just gets more complicated. The child fell on the playground and got hurt? There's nothing that a little piece of chocolate won't fix; lucky I've got one in my bag. She calms down so quickly that way, something sweet in her mouth, and the knee doesn't hurt anymore. Getting bored at the birthday party? Hey, there are always the bowls of chips and sweets to nosh. Boredom becomes less awkward with food, because when your mouth is chewing you're actually doing something, you're no longer in the experience of nothingness, you're no longer searching for an activity that will disperse the boredom; you're busy, you're experiencing pleasure, and the frustration is forgotten. And when the kids are fighting in the car? Let's just pull out a snack, preferably one that will last the whole journey, because when their mouths are busy they make less noise, and when their bodies feel comfort they fight less, so what if we can no longer survive a ride over to Grandma's house without a bag packed with food—while preparing it you feel really good about yourself, because preparing food for your children is always gratifying.

Gradually, the feelings of hunger and fullness aren't what they used to be, and the food makes its way into the emotional realm—and the most painful thing about it is that it happens because that's what we teach them. We introduced the emotional addiction because it was convenient, because it resolved a distress, because that's what we do, because it's hard to see your child frustrated or in pain, because food makes you happy, because we had the best intentions.

Somehow, we're okay with thirst. Most of us don't remind them to drink, don't make them drink water, don't tell them to finish their cup, and look—they're in perfect control of that, it doesn't go wrong, doesn't get mixed up with other things; it stays simple and, most of all, stays theirs instead of becoming ours.

And then comes the stage at which the most confusing voices are heard. A parent who has a child who is too fat or too thin is perceived as someone who fell asleep on duty. Those voices explain why it's your responsibility that the child eats more or less

and why it is your fault if other children laugh at him and determine that you were the one who failed if you walk around with a
chubby child. "Sure, the kid has no limits," they'll whisper behind
your back. "Why do they let her have a chocolate ice cream if they
can offer a popsicle instead?" "Now he's just four, but when he's
fourteen it will be too late." What these voices are actually saying: as parents, we are sometimes required to teach our children
to stop themselves and to set a limit, to bring them face-to-face
with an unwanted reality. So what's the difference between letting
her watch TV all day long and letting her have seconds at lunch?
Maybe we should intervene? Take responsibility where they still
can't? Maybe we are supposed to help them to be thin before they
comprehend the deep and dark meaning of not being thin?

We haven't said a word about genetics yet or about our own
eating disorders, about the fact that we may lecture and talk,
limit and educate, but at the end of the day, they know—they see
us standing at the kitchen counter wolfing down a fresh baguette
or eating a whole tub of ice cream while sitting in front of the
TV after a hard day. They feel our eyes when they eat too much
and our anxieties when they eat too little. They realize that the
contract has been broken, that we are now in their court, that
they may not be able to trust their bodies or themselves, that
they aren't good or pretty or thin or presentable enough for us,
that we've taken control of their bodies and they are not free, required to do nothing but obey. We tell them when they're hungry
and when they're full, when they feel like something sweet and
when it's time to stop.

We play a significant role in guarding the parameters of the
area: determining how many sweets we allow a day, putting a
meal on the table, having healthy food available at home, setting

an example (also a human example—showing them that we also have a hard time resisting once in a while, and cut ourselves some slack, or, on the other hand, win by managing to eat just one piece of chocolate, even though we felt like eating the whole bar), and teaching them the basic habits of eating healthy, getting exercise, enjoying a nice family meal focused on the conversation, togetherness, laughs, or a summary of the week, not on other people's plates, how much or how little they eat, not being allowed to get up from the table, threatening that they won't get dessert if they don't finish their plate, or numerous other damaging mistakes. And no, we shouldn't fill the house with sweet traps when there is a child dealing with the challenge of restraint, even if his siblings are thin and fit. And yes, we should teach them from a very young age that their body is smart and knows—it knows when they are tired, thirsty, when they need to go to the toilet, when they feel like something sweet or salty—and that they can count on their body.

When he turned around and said to me, "Mom, that was one of the saddest places I've ever been," I understood him. I had no doubt in my heart: I would go on searching until I found the conditions that would allow him to reach the goal he set for himself, because that's my job, because he sent out a distress call to the universe and I've been his universe for almost seventeen years. And in our contract, his job is to want, dream, improve, develop and my job is to listen to him—the crying, the calling out, the things that are said and unsaid—and help, encourage, count on him even when he still doesn't count on himself enough, believe that he can even when it's hard, let him encounter life as it is, with its gains and losses, with the wonderful and terrible genetics inside, with being whole and incomplete, just like me, and knowing that he is his own boss. I'm only here to be a universe that will respond to him.

When I ask myself why I choose not to look at their plates or comment when they take more, why I don't sit down with them for a chat and tell them they have to lose weight, my answer to myself is very simple: despite the will or fantasy of having the perfect family picture with thin, fashionable kids, despite the realization that in many respects it will even be easier for me to take charge of it, manage it, be the food policewoman, I choose to move aside and love them as they are without trying to fix them, improve them, criticize them, change them. Because to me, there are prices that I am not willing to let them pay. And yes, it's not an easy choice, but some of the coolest, happiest, smartest, and bravest people I know wear XL.

Today, one year later, he weighs seventy-five pounds less, size M. We found a dietitian who was wise enough to laugh at him a little, create a diet that would include all the things he loves to eat, and, especially, explain to him the meaning of patience and emphasize the rewards. We just stood on the sidelines and looked on in admiration, raising a toast to his determination and perseverance at family dinners. And after he lost ten kilos and no one at school said a word about it, we celebrated every extra hole in the belt that became unnecessary. Soon enough he realized he can go on without the dietitian and asked to release her and continue by himself. And exactly one year after we started, after a moving shopping spree, he suggested that we buy her flowers. We drove over to her house, him, me, and the bouquet. When I asked him on the way how he sums up the year, he said he feels that if he can say goodbye to the fat boy he used to be, then he can do anything.

forty-two

The Shaming Challenge

I T'S THE MORNING BEFORE A BIG LECTURE. THE CLOTHES were set out yesterday. I wake the kids up earlier than usual and quickly comb the girls' hair. Yuval is taking them to school today. I take another sip of coffee, go over the cards, leave the house on time, reach the university campus parking lot, take one last look in the mirror, fix a touch of smeared lipstick. Excited, always excited. A kind of pleasant and distressing alertness. I check the time. Ten more minutes. I play a song that puts me in a good mood, check the time again and leave the car. And then it happens.

I take the first step and something feels strange about the right shoe, a boot with a stiletto heel that has disappeared. With a pounding heart I open the car door again and there, next to the accelerator, it rests lifeless, my heel, which was probably worn out after five consecutive winters. In a desperate attempt, I try to wiggle the other heel, like in a commercial I saw for some sweets, where the cool girl just calmly bends over and yanks off—god knows how—the other heel, continuing to her work meeting in flats. "Never mind," I convince myself. "I'll just march ahead.

214

How hard could it be to imagine that the heel is still there? No one will notice."

The walk to the lecture hall feels like a never-ending trek. On the stage, I try to examine the expressions on the faces sitting in the front rows, to see if they notice anything out of the ordinary. Looks like they don't. The show must go on, the actress is determined, the audience doesn't notice, and the right leg gets used to the worsened conditions. But then, on the fourth sentence, while stepping carefully, I notice a change in the expressions and some whisperings of the women in the audience, who have noticed a black trail of sole crumbles I was leaving behind. The stage is covered in shoe pieces, and that very second, like clockwork, heel number two collapses and I with it.

The feeling of shame is very present in our adult lives, and much more so in our children's lives, almost from the first day they leave our house and head out to their first educational framework. A group of kids looking and whispering, getting chosen last in sports, giving the wrong answer and making everyone laugh, falling over in the yard and everyone turning to look, having your mother dress you in strange trousers and someone commenting about it in front of everyone, peeing your pants and everyone noticing, the children laughing at you because you're thin, short, nerdy, wear glasses, stutter, walk slowly, eat in a funny way, lose your tooth, get a haircut, and more. When the shame (or the shaming, call it as you like) meets our children out there, they feel as if the universe has stood still, as if all the TV screens in the world turn on and all the channels broadcast their humiliation. They turn into a mistake at that moment, and that mistake is hanging in the middle of the town square for everyone to see.

Judgment and criticism are qualities that are often glorified as "the intellectual's disadvantage," but when they become a method for education, when our home consistently is a place that takes on the role of critic, fixer, judge, we raise (with the best of intentions) children who grow up to be their own worst judges. In a judgmental, critical environment, shame flourishes. Children need to know what we know already: there is no one who isn't ashamed of something (assuming he's not a sociopath), because shame is part of being imperfect and being in ongoing communication with other imperfect human beings. The real courage is staying on the court, continuing to conduct ourselves well, being empathetic, noticing when someone else feels shame, forgiving ourselves.

The only way to raise children who are able to meet the shame challenge is to give up on criticism. And yes, allow yourself to be a little less perfect in front of them. Tell them about your own experiences and failures so that they feel more human. Tell them what you were thinking at that awful moment when you stepped into the men's room by mistake, that you thought the whole world was ridiculing you even though there was just one person in there. Tell them that when the people at work gossiped about someone, you joined in, but when you saw her crying in the corner later you walked up and said sorry. Reinforce them every time they are sensitive to other people's feelings and tell them what an important quality that is, because being sensitive is to feel, and whoever feels not only happiness and success but also frustration and shame is brave.

Remember that girls encounter shame through gender concepts that instruct them to be pretty, polite, good, perfect, to hide the fact that they broke a sweat on the way. Boys, on the other hand, encounter concepts that are related to strength—pity the boy who is considered weak. So let the girls be wild and less tidy, and let the boys be weak. Let them encounter themselves in a safe place, at home, with each of the characteristics that will bring them across the feeling of shame outside. Then, maybe, it will be easier for them to face all the social challenges that are waiting for them out there, including coming back home one day a few inches shorter because the heels on their shoes fell off in public.

forty-three

Beware of Competitiveness

FOR FIFTEEN YEARS SHE WAS BROUGHT UP LIKE A RACE-horse. Even her chestnut hair gleamed when she caught the scent of a competition. She was an expert at lunging forward when the whistle blew, focused on her adversaries and their location on the course, always the winner. When she was younger, her mother would start her and her siblings with the cry "Who's going to be first in the bath?" She remembered exactly how she would plan to push her older brother, how her body got pumped with adrenalin, how her little sister always cried when she won, how she felt when she mocked them, "Last one there is a rotten egg!" "And now," she said, "now look what's happened. I'm the rotten egg."

At fifteen, she lost for the first time, and her hair stopped gleaming. The boy she was interested in chose someone else. And not just anyone: he chose her friend, a golden, skilled Thoroughbred racehorse who trampled her on the way to victory. For six months she'd been busy licking her wounds, avoiding the race course. The excellent grades she had flaunted were gone, and she had dropped out of ballet even before that, realizing that genetics had betrayed her and without a willowy physique she wouldn't manage to become the best. And the girls who always surrounded her when she radiated power and success disappeared when they realized, she explained, that she was no longer leading anyone, barely herself. "I have nothing now. I lost the race," she concluded. "And there's no place in my heart for losers. Whoever loses is a rotten egg."

Because we live in a competitive world, we tend to think that we have to prepare our children for the competitions, train them to win, to aspire to achieve so they can survive. What we can't see is the shortcomings of this narrow worldview: there is no environment that is more destructive to the potential of a person's happiness than a competitive environment. In a competition, the contestants are forever evaluated on the basis of a single bottom line. No one asks them if they enjoyed the process, what their self-image is, if they helped anyone or learned something they didn't know. In a competition, only you exist—all the others competing against you, your enemies or people who are inferior to you, are of no interest—and the sum total of your value is limited to an extremely narrow shelf: the shelf of trophies, where there is only one first place.

Would you want to raise a child whose sense of worth, entire self-image, and experiences depend on a single bottom line? A child who sees everyone as potential enemies, who enjoys the thin and intoxicating air of victory but also feels the ground crumbling beneath her when she loses? A child who wastes so much energy and feels so much anxiety only because she's busy calculating her opponents' possible trajectories? Would you want to raise a child who will never know the sweetness and benevolence of being considerate toward someone else? Who doesn't know the magic that seeps into your heart when you give in and let a friend feel like a winner? There is a reason why they say "it's lonely at the top."

We may not have control over a competitive society, but we have plenty of control over how we perceive competitiveness. Paradoxically, the real winners in the race of life are those who learn to invest their energy in developing and progressing, not at the cost of others, but in relation to themselves. The ones who can ask themselves, and not just themselves, if they are happy, what's missing, what can be improved, what they can and can't relate to, what the next step might be. Because in such a place, far more energy is available to create human contact, an inner dialogue, to breed creative thinking, optimism, togetherness, self-love.

The next time you roar, "Let's see who finishes everything on their plate first!" or "Who's going to be ready for the bath first?" realize that what you're teaching them is rivalry, external instead of internal attentiveness, and lack of cooperation. And mostly, you're putting them on a path that might lead to a certain objective, but only one of them will come out with a sense of worth, and a provisional sense of worth at that, which will last only until the next time they lose. If you're really so desperate to get supper or the bath over and done with, pit yourself as their adversary. Group them together, and when you lose, sound that sense of losing out loud and tell them you feel like a rotten egg. Ask them if they could encourage you, remind you that there are other things you do really well, that a competition isn't always fair, that you shouldn't despair, and that it was fun trying. Tell them that maybe next time you'll all compete together against the clock, and then everyone will have fun, even if the clock wins, because when you have fun and help each other, you're always a winner.

Our reactions often reinforce the competition mechanism without us even noticing. Telling a child "Never mind, next time you'll win" actually emphasizes the bottom line that causes the suffering in the first place, instead of being with him in the pain of losing, telling him that it really feels bad, showing him (when he's younger) or asking him (when he's older) what he still managed to enjoy, what he did right even though he failed.

When you're having a political debate at the family dinner table, don't hold on to one truth: teach them to ask questions, to dispute another person's opinion but not dismiss it, to enjoy the debate itself even if they don't win the argument, so that the person next to them will not feel defeated. Say aloud that the winner in your eyes is the one who did the best job at listening to others while concentrating on her own argument, the person who brought up the topic of debate, learned and researched the issue, enjoyed the path, didn't get worked up even though she got mad, and didn't despair even though she didn't stand a chance.

In the example you set as a couple, too, think hard about whether there is any competitiveness there, because the kids are wonderful observers, especially of things that remain unsaid. So the next time your child is sick, instead of fighting over who will take the day off and reminding the other that you did it last time and that you're tired of having to always be the one who gives in, try to have a real discussion about cooperation, real needs, giving in, and being considerate. Even if it comes at a price, remember that you get to teach your kids something that's far more important than winning.

It's dangerous for a person's sense of worth to lean on just one foundation. In a world that is separated into winners and losers, children have only two positions through which they can evaluate themselves. The important parental task is to teach value and competence in a wide perspective that isn't limited to these two possibilities. This is the best preparation for the competitive world out there.

— forty-four —

My Ordinary Child

THE ALMOST PERFECT FOURTEEN-YEAR-OLD SITS IN front of me at the clinic, complaining about the gap she experiences between "almost" and "perfect." This gap is what drives her. If she just had a shirt like this, a phone like that, those Adidas sneakers, that gap might close. She talks about her grades in math, how she almost got a B minus. She said that in her opinion it might sometimes be better to fail than to get a B minus. When I asked why, she couldn't explain.

The last time we met, she told me she had dreams in which she started singing and suddenly this amazing voice came out. She was on a stage and all the people she knew were there, and she just sang, so effortlessly, so beautifully. But now, as she tells me about how awful she feels, it all comes together.

"Can you describe what's so awful about this?" I ask.

"You know . . . I'm just . . . so ordinary! I look ordinary!" she says, and as the word *ordinary* comes out of her mouth, her face twitches in disgust. This girl-woman's greatest fear is to be ordinary.

We all want to raise special children and give our children the feeling that they're special. Almost every child carries in her bag of happy memories a dance on the living room table, the cameras of family members focusing on her, and behind the cameras the sparkling eyes of a captive audience. All our children are stars when they're little—they're our stars and we are their skies. They shine and feel that embrace of specialness that they will always long to feel again. We talk to them about the future and promise them they can be whatever they want to be, and they imagine a giant tree of sweets—once they're tall enough, all they'll have to do is reach out and pick.

And then, gradually, life gets in the way. The kindergarten teacher doesn't always see how wonderful they are, their friends are busy promoting their own wonderfulness, the stage doesn't feel like it did before, and the audience doesn't arrive with gleaming, proud eyes. Sometimes the audience doesn't show up at all. And then come the big questions: Have we taught them how to cope with their ordinariness? Did we let them feel good even when the limelight wasn't on them? Did we teach them how to be a part, wait their turn, realize that their uniqueness doesn't go away even if no one is acknowledging it?

Being ordinary is a curse to that fourteen-year-old girl. It's gray, pointless, mediocre. Being ordinary is not standing out: not in the mirror, not by having a particular talent or by being clever, not even thanks to a certain frame of mind. Being ordinary is giving in. To her, it's sad.

But maybe being ordinary can be marvelous? Being ordinary is having inner peace, a profound sense of proportion and understanding of the relativity of life; it's realizing that everyone has something special about them, and the closer we get to them, the more we can discover in them. Being ordinary is realizing that we're all ordinary, even if some of us go around behaving as if we're something special. Being ordinary is realizing that working at being special is exhausting and pointless, and if we work on having fun, being true to ourselves, developing and learning and creating—we might be able to say goodbye to our fear of being ordinary.

Most of us think our children are wonderful. Sometimes they're also especially talented at something: singing, drawing, or playing an instrument or being clever, being talented at playing ball, or exhibiting a phenomenal knack for acting. But on the journey of life, the hard task they face is leading their life with happiness even when the spotlight isn't on them, even if they didn't get into the exclusive school that should have highlighted their super talent. To that end, we need to keep their self-image stable, consistent, and solid. If their contract with life is going to depend solely on the delightful sensation of uniqueness, anything less will hurt, even anger them. When they encounter their own ordinariness—and we are all ordinary, flesh and blood with a limited expiration date—all their motivation mechanisms will turn either toward avoidance or toward a stubborn and futile struggle to retrieve that sought-after sensation of being special. They will experience difficulties in the social sphere, at the end-of-the-year parties, as teenagers searching for an identity that is distinct from their captive audience; it will be difficult in relationships when the infatuation ends and the tedious routine kicks in, or at the workplace when they aren't praised or when their sense of significance isn't nourished.

We also have to address what this sense of uniqueness serves when it comes to us. We already know very well how ordinary we are, but then an especially beautiful, especially talented, especially special child comes along, and we feel that maybe through her we can get back on that stage again. And when she encounters rejection in life, we experience the greatest insult. We'll tell ourselves we're empathizing, that we're coming apart because our heart is aching for her, that we are fighting for her to get accepted to the school, course, musical show, or campaign, because it would be just perfect for her, but what we're actually doing is focusing on ourselves and teaching her that being ordinary is not an option. After all, we've invested so much in her uniqueness. And that's where the trouble starts—that will be the core of her own fears for years to come. She won't know why she can't be happy, why she has given up on so many sources of joy, and why her contract for satisfaction with life is so narrow and limiting.

It's important for us to realize the destructive potential of celebrating our children's uniqueness. Let's teach them the joy of routine, being a part of something, even the joy of failure. Let's not forget that our child's inner dialogue is in our hands, and the right inner dialogue is: "It's okay that I've failed or wasn't accepted, that they didn't play with me or didn't let me talk when I raised my hand, or that they weren't impressed by me. I can handle the feeling of ordinariness and still love myself or see the best in me without wasting energy on getting hurt, feeling angry, avoiding things, or tilting at windmills. I know who I am, and my feeling of being visible and my own sense of worth aren't threatened."

This doesn't mean we'll give up on the spark they light in our eyes and hearts—we'll go on celebrating them as they dance on our living room table to enthusiastic applause. But we will also shed light on the most ordinary qualities they possess and acknowledge these on a daily basis with plenty of appreciation. Because being patient, showing restraint, making an effort, showing determination, helping others, possessing a sense of humor, being a good listener—all these are what create strength and resilience in our children. And when the audience doesn't show up, and the spotlights don't turn on, we'll be there to applaud them, and then they might just be able to tolerate the wonderful sense of ordinariness life has to offer.

forty-five

Saving Them from Instagram

"EVERYONE HAS A LIFE, BUT I HAVE NOTHING, MOM! Understand? Nothing!" she concludes and moves to the evidence. She opens one of her apps: "Yesterday at two a.m.— two a.m., Mom!—two of my friends are hanging out together. And another one this morning: looking at the sea, holding a pink slushy. It says 'Life in pink' and there's an arrow pointing to the slushy." And then she shows me another photo of two friends at a café right next to our house; they had walked by and didn't bother to invite her to join; and another friend, who had texted her yesterday to say she didn't feel like celebrating her birthday, now appears on Instagram with balloons and two friends who came to surprise her. My daughter looks on from the sidelines at the life she isn't living today, opportunities she missed out on, parties and smiles, others' togetherness, and her aloneness, and it brings about awful thoughts: everyone is happy, everyone is having fun, but me. And her? She's probably not good enough, not pretty enough, not cool enough. One look at Instagram and the princess turns into a frog, but no one is searching for her with a glass slipper.

Adolescent girls' social sphere has always been ruthless. While boys get used to rejection, losing out, and loneliness at a tormenting but tolerable volume, most girls dive into a pool of jealousy, self-image issues, insulting innuendos, and social cruelty, which don't stem from evil but from the existence of layers on layers of sensitivity and vulnerability in interpersonal relationships. Today, with the social platforms that, at every moment, narrate stories whose cruel nuances can only be fully understood by an adolescent, the volume is amplified and becomes earsplitting.

If you try to understand what it's all about and check her phone, you'll find cute, cheerful pictures of adolescent girls having a good time. What the adolescent sees there, however, is all the moments she wasn't tagged, the insufficiently enthusiastic comments, the forever unsatisfying number of likes, and all the get-togethers she wasn't invited to. She looks through a window onto all the places where she isn't, and this window lets in harsh gusts. They create unnecessary storms at such a sensitive age, when it all comes to self-image, social presence, personal branding, and creating an identity.

But that window is already open and there is no adolescent girl we can shut away from the social platforms, and we also wouldn't want to stop them from coping with such a focal, daily element of reality, just as no one stopped us from leaving the house or meeting up with friends because "girls are mean and you're better off staying at home." But we do need to realize that coping is harsh and complicated, sometimes unbearable, and that there is a certain parental input we have to offer so we can live in peace with adolescence on Instagram and various other supposedly innocent and positive platforms that could even make girls who have no social difficulties miserable.

To understand the kind of pain they experience, imagine an app that sends you an alert every time someone is gossiping about you, with a highlight detailing the gossip. We haven't reached that point yet, but in the mind of a teenage girl, the incessant exposure to the social life of her friends is painful, incomprehensible, and injects regular doses of poison into her space. The parental task is not to disconnect her but to inject a sense of proportion into her little adolescent veins every day, to turn this social place into something you can talk about, try to understand, become immune to, and also agonize over together.

Important clarification: As in every parental task that is based on an educational agenda, there is nothing worse than when a parent starts a talk about gaining perspective when the teenager is in distress and originally came to tell her parent how terrible her life is and how offended she is by what the small screen shows her. In moments like these, we need to understand, listen, hug, tell her how insulting it is, how hard and confusing, and try to think together what could help her at that moment. Most of all, we should give her a feeling that there is a reason why she is feeling so awful, that anyone would feel the same in her shoes. Our perspective syringe comes into use in between, gradually, over and over, at other opportunities, as if we're irrigating a plant. We can inject perspective into the situation during a five-minute conversation, telling her about our own Facebook experiences or about a thought we had following a conversation (the next day, when she's already having a different experience), while showing an interest in her Instagram. Having lots of little chats with pervading messages slowly creates a framework of thought that could serve as a lifesaver for her on days of pain, loneliness, or worthlessness. External talk that can become internal. After a while, the next time she is in distress, we might be able to remind her of one or two points she already knows but has forgotten momentarily because of that painful insult.

In the meantime, following are things to keep reminding her about in between the difficult times.

Remember That You Forget

Other people's photos can bring so much negativity to the way we see ourselves. We adults also feel a twinge when we see our friends abroad, at a concert or restaurant, celebrating, meeting, inviting and being invited. The real trick to resilience is not to disconnect but to learn how to live with the disturbing background noise hummed to us by other people's successes and happiness. The realization that yesterday someone else looked at your photo and felt like an outsider, a failure, inadequate, can serve as a moral compass for regulating the level at which we buy the story we're supposedly seeing on the screen.

The Story the Pictures Tell Is Momentary

What a wonderful gift it is to be able to stop life at a given moment and stage happiness. How fun it is to sit in a café with friends, wait for the milkshake, and think about the cool Boomerang, video, story, or picture you're going to make together. Directing the joy of togetherness is a social activity in itself, but it's important to remember that after we've taken the pictures, we're also supposed to be together, experience the flavor, enjoy the chat almost as much as we enjoyed taking the picture. And maybe the truly best moments are the smiles that weren't directed at the camera? The sincere laughter, the mutual listening, the story a friend tells you? There is no evil in a make-believe, staged, photographed world. But if you remember that the important thing is the ability to enjoy a togetherness that doesn't involve a screen, you can be the girl who's not only fun to make a story with but also fun to be with.

Tell Yourself Your Own Story

Does the fact that a friend just got a new Adidas bag, looks amazing with a new filter, or is having a pink drink by the blue sea mean that you have nothing? All it means is that you are watching her display while not having pink juice, a new filter, or an Adidas bag. I know that when you look at someone else's moments of happiness you feel as if you have nothing, but don't let that get the better of you. I'm not saying that what you see is fake—they might be having a great time there. But you know what's definitely a lie? The thought you formulate that says you don't have fun or belong, are not beautiful or happy, have no new things, that says life is happening while you're just looking on from the sidelines.

Create a New Reality

Stop making up these little lies that make you hate yourself, and remember how wonderful and loved you are, how much fun it is to be with you, how big your heart is. How much you love to dance, draw, listen to music, braid your hair, play *Monopoly*, read books, spend time with a good friend. Put the screen to the side, choose one of the things that you like, just one, and do something that makes you feel good. When your heart is happy, the fact that other girl has an Adidas bag is far less painful.

forty-six

Fathers and Sons, Mothers and Daughters

I T ISN'T POLITICALLY CORRECT TO TALK PARENTING IN the gender context, but almost all parents have experienced the differences between girls and boys and the way children of our own sex make us tick, just because we are of the same sex. The cliché talks about the little love a mother has when she gets a boy, and how much fun it is to father girls. In our house, I'm good at confronting Yuval when he gives one of our boys a mouthful in a way that screams unawareness, and he mocks me from the side when our adolescent girl sets me off and I lose control, standing in front of her as if I was facing myself, or my mother, and all my weaknesses.

"Don't intervene," he says when I try to shed some neutral light on the way he's reacting to the boys, but what he's trying to say is "Let me have this gut reaction. I'm hurting right now, because I know what it feels like to be a boy and you have no idea. So let me have this lack of awareness, let me sound like my father, because right now I have no other way of conducting myself with him. Right now I'm focusing on myself and giving him a mouth-ful, because that way I just might manage to shatter the worrying premonitions I have about him."

Even if we've read all the parental guidebooks around and we think we're equipped with all the knowledge needed to raise happy children, the moment will come when we meet our own blindness. At that moment, we will react to an external occur-rence with a specific child in such an emotional way that if some-one looks at us from the outside they'll have no idea why our reaction is so extreme, why we can't let go and get the message across differently, why it isn't clear at that moment who's the parent and who's the child.

When we encounter ourselves at such extremes on these occasions, it offers an opportunity to become aware, realize that the volatile, disappointed, insulted, and over-angry reaction has nothing to do with the child and his actions, objectionable as they may be, but with a fragile encounter between us and our reflection, which is looking back at us and setting off reactions: reminding us of painful episodes in childhood, hidden fears, un-fulfilled wishes, voices from the past. And it will always be more painful for fathers facing sons and for mothers facing daughters.

These junctures pose a great opportunity to leave the wounds behind us and realize we've become overinvolved. This girl who has chosen to go out looking sloppy, who chews gum or is being rude, who isn't studying as hard for exams as I did at her age, who isn't functioning correctly in the social sphere, who leaves her towel on the floor no matter how many times we ask her not to, who listens to trashy music, who scares me, shames me, insults me—this child is just making me face myself, with my mother's reactions, with my wish of creating a little woman who won't make my mistakes or who will be an improved model of what I have become. Somehow, in the space between me and her, all my pains forever live, and it's out of this pain that I react. My reaction when her brothers exhibit the same behaviors is very different. I either laugh or make a little comment or have a rational, well-managed talk or just attribute it to adolescence.

When it comes to Yuval, on the other hand, the boys set off the negative emotions that he regulates so well with the girls and at work. If his son suddenly gives up too soon, isn't productive, ambitious, manly, independent, skilled, or assertive enough, or any other quality connected to Yuval's own frustrations, unresolved issues, or dreams he had for his boys, then the steam press and mortar and rage that had been bottled up so efficiently all these years come out. He won't let this kid give up, he won't raise loser, geeky, oversensitive sons. Especially because it's too painful for them and he mistakenly believes, just as I do when confronting the girls, that he has some control over it.

So it's sometimes worth listening to our partners, who aren't set off by the same pains we are, and detaching ourselves from the weights that are burdening us and that will burden our children for life. We can also think about how we conduct ourselves with the child who doesn't press our buttons to better understand where the sound and balanced reaction lies. In that reaction, we are probably better parents. There, we remember that no matter who they are, what their sexual orientation is, how beautiful, thin, successful, or sociable they are—we are here to accompany them, love them, be proud of them, accept them unconditionally. Because who knows better than we just how much pain there is in a place where a mother didn't accept her daughter or a father didn't accept his son, how many scars such emotional experiences leave. It could be so liberating if we weren't an extension of anyone's dreams.

I think that only after twelve pregnancies and five children did I finally realize that I was having all the children that my mother had so wanted to have but couldn't. When I felt that even five wasn't enough, I realized that her hole would always exist within me. I don't like my hair down because she couldn't stand it like that; and I always think I could have done better, could be tidier, thinner, smarter, because I see myself through her eyes. Almost every night, when I go to sleep, I ask myself—if she were here, would she be proud? Would it be enough? What else can I do to be that girl she wanted so badly? It could have been much easier if she was just unconditionally proud of me.

forty-seven

Timeless Quality Time

I T SOMETIMES FEELS AS IF SUMMER IS THE SEASON OF memories. The hot weather inevitably sets the parental system into "memory production" mode: amusement parks, nature trails, vacations abroad—a blessed and well-planned escape from the routine that is well photographed and documented, forming a significant piece in our kids' inner puzzle. We set out with plenty of good intentions and a big question looming over us: Will we manage to be that family that conducts itself pleasantly through the July–August heat, laughing out loud at meals and taking wonderful pictures against the backdrop of the mountains or the sea?

In reality, the memory splits into two scenarios:

~ What really happened, I: She spilled her drink again at the restaurant, and we had no change of clothes; the bill was outrageous; Yuval and I shared one dish; the disgruntled teenager on duty didn't enjoy his food and made sure we were aware of it; they fought over who would sit where; she wouldn't give him a bite and he mumbled that she was stingy and horrible, so a fight started, and they settled a twelve-year-old account; the little one had to use the toilet three times (two were made-up, because she probably realized that going alone with Mommy to the toilet equals quality time). But, hey, at least I didn't cook and didn't have to clean up after them. A dreamy vacation.

~ What really happened, II: When the drink spilled, I looked at Yuval, sighed, and smiled (he smiled less); I put a comforting hand on the knee of the teenager who complained about the food, and when the other one started fighting with his sister, I added in a few more childhood memories of deprivation and hatred, but really funny ones, and that took the fun out of the war they had started; between taking the little one to the toilet and fighting over the seats, I asked each one of them what they had enjoyed most so far, and when it was my turn, I told them that I was having the best time now. This is just how I am—a woman without a past and without a future, only the present. Enjoying myself in the now. How important is it? We started a philosophical debate about the meaning of the present compared to the past and future and explained to the little one what the past is; I looked at us all from the side, all the blunders and imperfections, and smiled on the inside, and then the check came. "Let's make up a swear word in our own language for every time a really big check arrives that wasn't worth the meal," I suggested, and they made up lots of new swear words. I laughed (Yuval laughed less), and until the waiter came back with the change, I asked to sit beside their father and explained that sitting next to him was better than dessert, it was my sweet something. They made room for me, and then the little one really did have to go to the toilet.

Childhood memories are the most subjective and complex mosaic that exists inside us. The things we remember, the things we have completely forgotten (but our siblings remember very well), the ones that were reinterpreted over the years—these become a part of who we are, accompany us when we become parents, hurt us, hug us. They include smells, tastes, touches, music; parents arguing, family trips, relationships between siblings, dinners, holidays. If in our childhood experience there was pleasure, warmth, comfort, and fun, we can set out on life with a positive outlook. If the children we used to be had a negative experience, fear, pressure, anxiety, stress, or sadness imprinted, we might have a hard time creating a different interpretation in the future.

The summer is just an excuse, a blessed excuse, to put our crazy lives on hold for a week or two and be in the present. It doesn't matter if we passed through the security check at the airport, went to Disneyland, stayed with Grandma and Grandpa, spent a week together at home, or went to the beach or supermarket—ultimately, the only thing we have any control over is our "experiencing self." We have no control over their "remembering self" or over a drink that was spilled or a fight that started. Our greatest responsibility is to tell them what they see in the picture: Who is that family having a meal in a mediocre restaurant? What is its value? What's not worth wasting energy on (scolding, threatening, telling them how hard we worked so they could enjoy themselves)? Who are they (people who are fun to be with, even though sometimes they're really not)? And it's when things go wrong that our greatest "memory test" as parents comes along—this is where the autopilot is impressed in their memories, where you determine how they react when their own children spill their drinks. Because the most significant memories are not necessarily the ones we remember but those that dwell in us without us even knowing.

Good memories are created when we have the ability to be in the present and choose to remember only the pleasant things: to control our interpretations, to make sure that the expectations that arise from a brochure depicting a dreamy green meadow and beds with white sheets are kept in check, and to order ourselves not to lose it, but instead to have fun, enjoy a conversation with our child on the way to the elevator, look at them sleeping side by side or having conversations they wouldn't usually have, try on clothes we would never buy in a shop where no one knows us, laugh, a lot, about everything that doesn't succeed or work out, sing in the car together. To be a bit more of the kid who experiences and remembers, and a bit less of the parent who plans and gets disappointed.

Memories are not formed only in the summer. Our children are equipped with receptors for every sensation of pleasure that comes their way all year round. And here we reach the familiar term *quality time*, which is usually accompanied by unnecessary expenditure: shopping at the mall, eating at a restaurant, visiting an amusement park, or having one afternoon every week that is dedicated to some activity that brings us closer. Even though I'm totally for any value system that assigns mutual time to a parent and child away from day-to-day worries, why do we actually have to create a particular activity with the people who mean the most to us in the world and mark it in our calendar as if it was a strategy meeting at work?

The whole idea of being a child is enjoying the moment, indulging the inability or lack of will to plan, preferring "I want" to "I should." When they're still young, we allow this, let them experience the moment, because it's obvious to us that playing is important for development, that laughing out loud is healthy, and that covering yourself in mud is fun. But when they join an educational system, that contract changes: the important playing is pushed in between picking them up from school and practicing letters and numbers at home, and if we're really efficient, they might manage to fit in a short hour of playing, which is often substituted for some screen time, because we also need to fit that in.

The idea of quality time is an unfortunate side effect of a culture that lacks spare time. It is the result of a set of cultural values that require us to do what we must and only then to find time for what we want. It is a concept intended to launder the guilt feelings of absent parents with the help of a goal-oriented cover whose message is: spend time with your child, charge her battery, remind her that she's important to you, and remind yourself that sometimes it's nice to spend time with her.

But the fact is that quality time with the kids is far simpler than you think. It's made of short moments when you put the phone down, postpone writing that email, doing the laundry, making dinner, cleaning up, and other tempting tasks, and put it into words: "Hey, Yoavi, do you have a few minutes to sit with me?" "Shira, I've got to ask for your advice on something that happened at work." "Rona, come keep me company while I prepare dinner and we'll have a little chat, just you and I." The emphasis in the verbalization has to be on the "You and I, together, alone." This time can take place alongside the other siblings, as part of your daily routine; there is no need for special expenditure or creativity in dreaming up ideas, and there's also no need to upload a photo together captioned with "Time with Mommy."

Pushing your nose into your four-year-old's ear and asking her to do the same, giving it a name, and laughing because it tickles—that's quality time. Driving in the car with your adolescent and asking him to play a song he likes through the speakers (instead of his headphones) and then laughing about the fact that it is not your kind of music, but that you're so lucky you have him and this song and that you're in the car together because otherwise you'd feel even older—that's quality time. Asking for your ten-year-old's advice when you've been insulted by someone at work and can't decide what to do about it and really listening to him and telling him that his solutions are the best—that's quality time. And arranging oranges on the table and giving them the names of children from kindergarten, telling her about something you read today and asking her what she thinks about it, just sitting on the couch together, painting your nails together, or jumping in a puddle—all quality time.

A lot of things that we do with our children spring from a desire to create memories—we really want them to remember that trip, that day off, the crazy event we organized for their birthday, or the day they got their report card. But the truth is that the most significant memories aren't of events or parties; the real memories dwell in a sensory, emotional place that is without words and certainly without credit cards or piles of presents. The memories that become a part of who they are, that stitch together the parents they become, and that determine the kind of partners they will look for can be found in a place of real, quiet, intimate presence; of touch, exchanged glances, the scent of each other's bodies, and the aromas of cooking; of unpretentious togetherness that isn't timed, isn't written down on the calendar; the simple opposite of quality time.

forty-eight

Old-School Parenting

"PARENTS TODAY ARE AFRAID OF BEING PARENTS!" "Parents are scared of their own children!" "There is no parental authority these days!" "We're raising spoiled children. We compliment them incessantly and are then surprised when they're still living at home at twenty-five." These are the declarations that guide the best parenting specialists in the Western world today and that naturally make parents feel even more lost, directing them straight into the arms of a system that will reeducate them about how to be parents. "Take the screen away from him!" "Look her straight in the eye and let her know who calls the shots in this house!" and other recipes for good parenting and raising successful, happy, and polite children who are disgusted by porn and drugs and who love to do the dishes and pay for school supplies from their own pocket money.

When I see lots of exclamation marks, lots of question marks instinctively pop up in my mind. Maybe we've become a little confused? Maybe we're so preoccupied with ourselves, work, loss of our fantasies, financial pressure, the ongoing attempt to keep several balls in the air that we've forgotten that parenting is actually a very elementary thing?

All in all, our own parents' parenting wasn't too bad. Some might claim that it wasn't too good either, but no one can argue about the fact that there was far less confusion on the parental front back then. The formula was more or less the following: Life is hard; kids are not at the top of our priorities list; once in a while you need to set a child straight and the rest of the time it's totally fine if they roam around without us knowing exactly what's going on with them. Furthermore, school is important, so is brushing your teeth; you don't argue with teachers and you eat until you're full. This formula didn't address veganism, gluten-free, organic vegetables, and a balanced diet. A child's subjective world, her emotions and thoughts, learning disabilities and social challenges, made parents lose sleep only in very extreme cases.

And we grew up. Somehow, we grew up. We got dirty and bruised; we were a little intimidated by our parents; when we were lost or confused, no one was there at the other end of the line; we had simple bedrooms with posters hanging on the wall from the only teenage magazine available; we shoplifted from the grocery store; we didn't always do our homework; and we walked a lot. We were kids. And we were sure to brush our teeth, listen to our teachers, spend a lot of time outdoors, and pay attention every time our parents were cross with us or set us straight.

No, it's not the same these days. There is a generation gap, and a culture of excess and new technologies and an influx of advisers and clinicians. And all this alongside a need and pressure to raise beautiful, smart, and talented children, the kind we can showcase on the victory shelf of our lives, next to the beautiful house, spotless car, impressive title, booming career, and photos from our exotic vacations. And still, there are some old-school principles that have withstood time and are worth preserving.

Children Should Climb Trees

I spent the first years of my childhood in a quiet neighborhood in Haifa, in northern Israel. In first grade, I walked to school alone. It took half an hour with my short legs. On the way home, my friends and I would stop over in the forest to look for snakes and climb one especially low pine tree, the sap sticking to our knees and fingers. We would throw stones into the valley and then hurry home, because an inner clock told us that our mothers were already waiting for us at the window, upset about us being late and then also about the sap stains that don't come out in the wash. The thing I liked best was to go on adventure trips, touch tadpoles swimming in green ponds; and when we played football on Saturdays, Dad always called me "Courage."

But these days, when the activity mat has replaced the good old floor and carpet, and playgrounds no longer have sand and old car tires, we should remember that there's nothing like scraping your knees, tearing a hole in your pants, putting a really disgusting plant in your mouth, and even burning your feet a little on a hot sidewalk. Before you get too horrified and wrap your little loved ones in bubble wrap again, remember that childhood is all about climbing trees, because the confidence and risk management they learn doing that are worth the scratches. Childhood is all about burning a dry leaf with a magnifying glass in the sun, because it teaches them something and requires patience and precision. Childhood is all about preparing a potion that might spill over or explode because of an amusing or unsuccessful chemical mix, depending on your point of view.

Children who take small but challenging risks taste the flavors of independence, confidence, and curiosity. Be there when they're climbing up to another branch, and look at them looking down, feeling on top of the world only three feet off the ground. What their smile reflects is mostly the confidence you gave them when you let go, the faith they have in themselves, in overcoming their fears.

You Don't Really Have to Know Everything

I never told my mother that I was caught lying in kindergarten and that the image of my kindergarten teacher, who was merciless and told me off in front of the whole class, will forever live on in my memory. If I had told her, I'm pretty sure her look would have clarified that she was actually happy I was caught lying, because "That's just how it is—that's the price of lying." She also didn't know that Osnat and I put on fashion shows in my room, and that sometimes, when we were in an especially whimsical mood, we would do it naked. I also didn't tell her that our family friends' daughter, who was two years older than me, taught me how to French kiss while our parents were chatting in the living room, eating dip, and thinking that the children were playing nicely. I didn't tell her lots of other things, but I always knew exactly what my parents would think and how they would react if they had known. Today we are told that we're supposed to spy on our children, check their phones and question them methodically, not forgetting to add diverting questions about things we already know, just to check their credibility.

Today, every story that starts with "he didn't play with me in kindergarten today" ends in a conversation between the mothers, a report to the kindergarten teacher, and an announcement on

social media "to see if it happened to any other children." What
we have to remember is that our kids are now in the midst of a
learning process that we have already completed. She is coming
across a child who doesn't want to play with her for the first
time, and the last thing she needs is a hysterical reaction from us
or for us to solve her problem for her. It belittles her and weak-
ens her, and our interrogations and overreactions teach her that
whatever happened was terrible. She'll come across a few other
children who won't want to play with her in her life, and sometimes she'll be the one who doesn't want to play with someone
else. She needs her private space, free from your invasions.

It's enough to ask her how she felt, whether she was more
angry or hurt, whether she felt as if she wanted to cry or to shout
at the other child that it wasn't nice. Give her the confidence of
knowing that it will gradually hurt less and that she'll know what
to do. After all, why should you know what the best solution is
for her? You and not her? And she's such a smart kid and has such
excellent solutions to so many problems.

And what about the dangers online and the wolves lurking
in online groups? More than anything, these things mark out our
unequivocal duty to conduct the most open and interesting conversations we can with our kids. Yes, those conversations that are
a real drag and that we could spare ourselves if we only had the
code to their phone and could read their every chat. Try to imagine being in a couple's relationship in which you had to check
your partner's phone once a day to see who he was texting, what
he was watching online, how he expressed himself—thinking hard
about whether you might have missed out on something funda-
mental. True, it's hard work to maintain a good relationship with
the children, having embarrassing or unpleasant conversations

with them sometimes, thinking how to get your point across when you're talking about appropriate behavior online. It's hard but much more constructive than prying into their lives after they go to sleep under the pretext of protecting them from danger.

Also, remember that if you've already gotten into the cops and robbers game, they will simply learn to hide things that they would have gladly shared with you if it wasn't for the game. Spare them the criticism, punishments, and hysteria, and prove to them that you're worthy of being their partners when they get stuck or screw up and that you can learn together from each mistake. Remember that part of the story of separation—that separation from you that they are supposed to undergo—is *not* telling you everything, leaving a little to themselves when they are younger and a lot when they're older. But if the relationship is a good one, you will earn the privilege of being the first person they call when they get into trouble. And that's far more important than knowing everything about them.

Children Aren't Supposed to Be Pleased All the Time

I hated going with my parents on errands and waiting in the car. I felt like an unlimited parking meter—there was no air conditioning, no clock, no end in sight. I hated it because there was a boredom to it, an endless staring at a corner of the upholstery that was coming apart, waiting for Mom or Dad to come back already from the grocery, bank, or plant nursery. And when they did get back, there was never anything in their bags that would make a child happy, just what they needed to buy.

The little slap, which was used on a daily basis in the past, has, I'm happy to say, long since gone extinct. But let's think for a moment about the parent who used that painful tool, taking into account that their child wouldn't be happy, would even feel hurt and humiliated—it was clear to this parent that the child should and could withstand the pain, while facing a significant authoritative-educational figure, in order to learn a lesson in behavior that would help him in life.

Today, we are light-years away from this approach—we want happy children and try to raise them with as little frustration as possible. We're alarmed when they are angry, quickly remove obstacles from their path, solve problems for them, buy, organize, have fun, spoil—everything in the name of happiness. But we are in fact wrong and especially misleading in this. The contract of "I'll give you anything you want and you just be happy" is a deceptive contract that is destined to create miserable people who are certain that the universe's job is to provide them with everything they want. Don't be surprised if at thirty-three they still can't understand why they aren't make a living just by watching YouTube and eating pizza, or why happiness just seems to get further and further away.

The right contract is "I'll give you exactly what you need, and you will learn to be happy." They are not supposed to agree with our boundaries; they're also not supposed to fully understand them. They are entitled to hear a rational and respectful explanation to every parental decision made in their environment, and then they are supposed to encounter a parent who completely accepts the fact that they are not pleased, even understands how angry or frustrated it makes them. But this shouldn't affect this parent's ability to calmly and assertively, without spanking, impose the fact that now is the time to take a shower, go home, ride with a helmet, or stay away from drugs. Our children are not supposed to be pleased, but they have the full capacity to be happy. Because that muscle, of being happy, is best trained when they have to deal with an unwanted reality, and it is used less when we offer them redundant services and take charge of their happiness as if it were our own.

Children Need Their Parents at Home

My mother, who was a school counselor, was always at home when we got back from school. She was so at home that to me she was home itself, as obvious as the kitchen and the rooms. She was there for us. Sometimes, I was a little jealous of the children with a key hanging around their necks who would go home to an empty house. It seemed like an exciting adventure to walk into an empty house. From four onward, Rani would shout every few minutes, "Mom, when's five o'clock?" and Mom would always give the exact answer. At five, when Dad finally came home, it felt as if a year had passed since lunchtime.

One of the most significant costs of feminism, capitalism, and success in the modern era is the lack of parental presence. The lack of joint time together, empty time, family boredom time. In the past, mothers would have a part-time job at most, which would bring them home at lunch to serve a hot meal, chat, help with homework, put the radio on in the kitchen, put another load of laundry in, and spend plenty of valuable time together. When the fathers would come home from work, straight to the family supper, they wouldn't be stuck writing emails or holding a conference call, but would, at most, watch the evening news. The houses were smaller, most of us shared a shower, room, or brushing our teeth with someone, and the accumulated weight of spending time together made the importance of family unequivocal.

It's of course wonderful that fathers are more involved in rearing children and that children can witness their mothers' gratification from work, but one thing has to be clear: nothing can replace the presence of a parent in the house. There is no real way of educating children and maintaining a good and deep relationship with them when we see them for two hours a day while we're finishing things off before our next workday. It's nice that we compensate once a year with a fun family holiday and tell ourselves that we're working so hard and that it's just what everyone needs, but there is nothing like the presence of a parent. Even when the adolescents are busy with their own things and the little ones are playing outside, even when they just open the door and step into the house. Make the effort and try to spend a little more time at home and to be present when you are there.

forty-nine

Divorce—Catastrophe or Crisis?

"**Y**OU KNOW WHAT DIVORCED KIDS ARE?" HE ASKED, a six-year-old sitting in my clinic, drawing with his four-year-old sister. He didn't look up, just went on drawing a black cloud on the backdrop of the blue sky he had painted earlier, when they both told me about going to an amusement park with their grandma. "Divorced kids are kids whose parents are divorced," he explained.

"Why are the kids divorced?" I asked.

"Because no matter which house they sleep in at night, they always feel as if they've been kicked out of the house they're not sleeping in."

I poured some juice into two small glasses and asked his sister what she was drawing.

"A family," she replied shyly.

On her page there were four lines surrounded by a circle.

When parents decide to get a divorce—and it doesn't matter if they are doing it out of a friendly understanding that it isn't working, being tired of fighting and going to couple's therapy, burning hatred, inconsolable breach of trust, raging jealousy, or any other emotion from the range of the most toxic emotions around—they are usually at a personal breaking point.

They usually know about the bit of having "the talk" with the kids from movies or a short guidance session they took, and they know to be careful, to bring the kids into the living room and to tell a quiet story about a great love that has ended, friendship that remains, and a love for them that will stay forever. It wouldn't occur to them to sit there and tell the story of how one of them was unfaithful, the years gone by without touching each other, the unsettled accounts that just kept accumulating, the love that was replaced with disgust. And while they're breaking the news to their kids, that they are breaking up their household, they hope to prove to them that divorce isn't the end of the world.

Divorce, if handled wisely, really isn't the end of the world. It doesn't have to be a catastrophe; it can just be a crisis, even one that will, in the perspective of time, foster strength and power in everyone involved. But let's not forget that from the kids' point of view, divorce is the end of their family—of their house, the bed they sleep in at night, their confidence, their life, their whole world. And the big difference—a huge one—between catastrophe and crisis relies on our ability as parents to be there on duty. Day after day, hour after hour, minute after minute, a divorcing couple have to prove to them that the death of the couple's love has nothing to do with them, that they are not part of the mutual mudslinging, that they don't have to pick sides, and, most of all, that their parents are willing to rise above their personal crisis and be functioning parents for them at all times.

And it's hard.

One of the greatest dissonances in this situation is between a parent's emotional state and the front they are required to put on for their children. It's almost impossible for a broken, angry, sad, or jealous parent to go on behaving as if it's business as usual on the parental front—after all, the kids will sense what one parent feels about the other parent even if he or she says nothing. We're not robots, we're just human, and we're having a hard time and feeling angry and have just lost our relationship. But the witnesses of our hardship are our children, who are more dear to us than anything, and we have to remember that our main job is to be there for them. This is where the most significant part comes in, the one that requires real superpowers.

When the children watch us dealing with a crisis, they learn mostly from everything that is unsaid (for example, our way of coping) and are hurt mostly by what is said (for example, every time we get them involved in our bickering). They learn what courage is if we take care of ourselves and create a new reality that is not self-righteous or accusing. They learn optimism if we manage to be happy with them even when we're having a hard time and crying at night. They learn to take responsibility and deal with an unwanted reality if we collect ourselves and solve the specific problems instead of accusing each other. And they crash if we ask them to take sides.

Asking the children to take sides is, for example, telling them that Daddy didn't transfer the money on time. It's deciding, in a moment of weakness, to tell them "the real story" because you feel that they're angry at you while they're supposed to be angry at the other side. It's using them as a weapon to hurt those who hurt you and mumbling sentences like: "You're so irritable when you come back from your Dad's place" or "Why does she dress you like that?" or "Of course he lets you. I always have to be the bad one" or "Mom is always late to pick you up." Every time you settle accounts with your partner and know that the children are the ones paying the price for it, you're forgetting that you have a parental role to fill, that you swore to them life would go on, that everything would be okay, that the family would remain as it was, just in two houses, and that your job is to prove to them that the pain they're feeling is tolerable, one they can live with.

As is, they're investing most of their energy in figuring out why this happened to them, adjusting to moving around every few days, missing a different parent every evening, and realizing that birthdays won't be the same, and neither will weekends and holidays. They need their remaining energy to survive, to move on. And every time you bring them into your grief or anger, you take away the energy they so desperately need.

Everyone makes mistakes. Mistakes are a part of life. We're not supposed to set an example of perfect people who don't make mistakes, because then the children will expect themselves not to make mistakes, and life will be much harder. It's just like learning how to pour a drink into a glass: they need to know that it will spill at first, that it takes time, that it isn't pleasant, but that it isn't too bad either, and that we learn to pour better with time. They'll learn to live with the mistake and the frustration, forgive themselves, and remember that it could always spill again. But shame on the parent who spills a drink and expects the child to be the one to clean it up and, at the same time, to comfort that child that everything is fine and will be taken care of. *We're* supposed to be there for them when their drink spills; they're not supposed to be there for us.

Especially not when they're little, especially not when they're hurting.

Profound differences in opinion about children's upbringing also exist in family units that are intact. When I see my husband making a dreadful mistake with one of the children, I bite my tongue and do my best not to intervene, realizing that he, too, is their parent and I have to let my children deal with him, even if that means getting hurt (assuming it's not a life- or soul-threatening situation). And then, when the hurt child comes to me, I listen to her story, understand her feelings were hurt, try to find out with her what can be done—but I would never start a coalition with her and turn her father into the bad guy who just gave her an unreasonable punishment, who never sees the good side, who fails and makes mistakes at the expense of the child victim. My parental task is to let my child express her insult, to understand it; but to really protect her, I can't take sides, because then she becomes little, weak, and in need of saving, while her father becomes a much greater monster than he really is. In the evening, after we get everyone into bed, I'm more than welcome to argue with him and tell my husband that I will not have him talk, behave, or conduct himself that way with the children, not because I assume we have to be exactly the same, but out of an understanding that we have mutual red lines in the process of raising our children.

The consoling part is that life really does go on after the family is torn apart. You have the ability to create a better, more complete, and safer reality for your children. And in it they will be able to overcome and realize that they aren't divorced, that life goes on, that they haven't lost a parent and haven't lost themselves—they're just dealing with a crisis. With good parents, coping is hard but tolerable, painful but empowering. Because our children, who didn't take any wedding vows with us, are actually the ones who will always get the improved version of us, the one wrapped in good intentions, able to rise above everything, to divert the focus from ourselves to really see them. The wound in the heart of the family that once was can go on influencing a child's whole life from a bad and painful place, but it can also be nothing more than a crisis that ends with acceptance and a clear certainty that life is wonderful all the same. It's totally in your hands.

fifty

A Guide for the Bad Mom

A T THE END OF THE DAY, DARK CLOUDS OF DOUBT creep in. "You're not enough," they say. Not patient enough, not attentive enough; you don't play, laugh, pay attention, show interest enough. I think about each one of the children, trying to remember what went on between us today, and all I can think of is uninteresting details: I dropped off, picked up, served. I don't remember the eyes meeting, can't remember a conversation or a smile, just technicalities, particular crises: we looked for her geometry homework exercises while she screamed hysterically that it was the end of her, adding a few more things I couldn't understand because she was speaking so fast and so unclearly lately, and when I have no patience, when I'm a bad mom, I don't even bother to find out what she's trying to say, but just pretend to understand, carefully making the right movements, like a soldier in a minefield.

What else was there today? Another sugar crisis with the little one. If I hear one more "Mom, is there something sweet?" I think I really might finally lose it. And no, I don't have a boundary issue, but the child just has to ask that question at least once an hour, regardless of the answer she gets. Sometimes I think it's her way of starting an argument. She already knows what the answer will be. It's as if once an hour she walks up and says: "Mom, I've got to feel significant, in control, present, so what will happen now is that I'll ask you for something sweet, you'll say I've already had something sweet, I'll hate you like I've never hated anyone in my life, and then I'll get angry, start insulting you, crying, screaming, arguing, promising that I won't ask for anything sweet for a week. You'll smile and still say no, and then I'll shout even louder and tell you you're a really bad mother, and that you don't care that your child is sad, and you'll take a deep breath and say nothing, just smile, and then maybe I'll throw a few things around too, to turn it into a real sound and light show. After about twenty minutes, I'll calm down, you'll hug me and whisper in my ear that you love me, and half an hour later we'll start all over again. Cool?"

When I'm a bad mom with the little one, I turn on the TV, glue her to the screen to get a bit of a rest from her. On days like that, even the clock takes revenge and it takes three whole hours to go from five to six. Time looks at me contemptuously from the kitchen wall, the television, the phone, not moving, stuck with the TV soundtrack. "Are you really a parents' counselor?" My thoughts are painted fifty shades of dark gray. "Just look at yourself. Shame on you!"

I try to remember what went on with the boys today. The eldest one said something about an exam and I said I'm dying to see it, just busy, and he folded back into his room. The other one asked for money to get an ice cream with friends. I was happy he was going out, because I was just dealing with the little one's sugar crisis, and I asked him to get some bread too, but I didn't even see his eyes, didn't ask how school was, or maybe I did ask, but the bad mom can't remember what he said.

The dark clouds make my insides turn when I try to think about the fourth one, the one who's always okay, who never makes any dramas. She's happy, kind, she's fine. "There's nothing fine about it, you bad mom," I lash out at myself. Of all of them, she had to be the one to get a mouthful in the morning when she couldn't find her school pullover and we were almost late. "Just take something already," I stepped all over her. "What's up with this pullover? Do you think I can know every waking second where all of you keep all your stuff?" I addressed her using *you* in the plural. She didn't talk back. She always stays in line, even when she's out of line. And me? I'm a bad mom today. Today, I'm a bad mom.

On the days when you're a bad mom, you won't get a hug. No one will look at you and say, "Come on, girl, *this* is being a bad mom? You really are your own worst enemy. And the bad one inside you? There's nothing bad about her—tired, exhausted, human, yes, having a bad day maybe. So why are you being bad to yourself too now, for the sake of poetic justice? You were a little less good with the kids today? You even sucked? Big deal."

You have to realize—only really good moms feel like bad moms. It's the cleverest feedback system in the universe, and it's the one that allows us to develop, understand the challenges of parenthood in depth, and yes, sometimes come down on ourselves, feel that we completely blew it or are just out of sync. It's part and parcel of being a good mom. The best.

We can assume that all the different kinds of moms are within you: the soft mom, the funny mom, the easygoing, patient mom; the one who can fix the toilet while handling a crisis at work;

the one who drives the kids around, has a good word to say, has boundaries. and treats every child individually. You're the mom who can tidy and do the laundry, remember to bring a peeled potato to school tomorrow, and also the one who gets tired, annoyed, forgetful, self-concentrated, who loses it, shouts, feels sorry for herself, cuts corners, and occasionally puts a toddler in front of the TV.

If the job of parenting were an easy job, we'd all be good parents all the time, and they, our pets, would be especially happy to see us, ask for little, be easily gratified, and only raise a flag when they were hungry or physically uncomfortable. The rest of the time we would stroke them, receive and give love, maybe even throw them a ball to fetch in the park. Raising human beings is a complicated business. Lots of conflicts are involved, urges, inner struggles, and, most of all, little people who gradually develop their own wants and needs and form their own personality, which grows in your space and with you but isn't always what you had in mind and doesn't always have a positive impact.

We're also human beings. We were also raised with plenty of good intentions, mistakes, hardships, and loneliness, and that's what it's like among people—the most intricate mission will forever be survival, the victory of good over evil. The little achievements are a display of great bravery, and the good parent is the one who possesses the inner criticism that helps her get up the next morning with the best intentions and the determination to beat the bad parent who also dwells within.

You are the Sole Survivor. Imagine yourself at the end of the day wearing a bandana with your tribe's name on it—your family name. Stop kicking yourself out of the game just because you feel you had a bad day. Remember that we're all struggling to be a little less bad but neglecting the battle of being less bad to ourselves. Blow away the dark clouds you created to let the sunshine in, and don't linger on mistakes. Say goodbye to the fantasy of being perfect, because it creates miserable children, and remember that tomorrow is a new day on your island.

I'm a good mom. I'm writing this to subdue the bad mom who lives inside me. I'm a good mom because I love each and every one of my kids the way they are; I can look at each one of them and understand they are doing what they are doing in order to grow and develop. I can release my expectations from them for the sake of their liberty to be who they are. I'm a good mom because I'm not afraid of being bad sometimes, because I give up on so many of my own needs for them, and because there are some needs I'll never give up on for them. I'm a good mom because I see the good in them, because I feel them, and because I let them be less good. I'm a good mom because I know exactly when I'm being a bad mom.

fifty-one

Eighteen Things I've Learned in Eighteen Years of Motherhood

I'M MAKING THIS LIST FOR MYSELF AND FOR MY CHILDREN so that when they enjoy the privilege of becoming parents and encountering the complexity of this role, they will read these words and maybe better understand themselves. Maybe they'll realize that the confusion you feel at eighteen doesn't go away at eighteen, and that life is full of contradictions and opposites even at forty-five.

1. Good parents don't expect perfection

You may think you've given birth to a tabula rasa on which you can paint your own masterpiece. You may think that if you're good enough parents, your children will be perfect people, but children aren't cars fresh out of the factory. They arrive with small scratches, sometimes with frame damage, and even when they seem flawless to us, at some point we discover the first dent and immediately mourn it and try to fix it.

I haven't met a perfect person yet, but I've met plenty of complete people, and every time I meet a complete person, I think that that person probably had very good parents: parents who were sure to refuel on time, who saw the scratches and realized that the flaws are less important than the journey, who didn't expect the perfect and as a result didn't go to the garage to fix dents, who looked at the image of their own imperfection reflected back at them through their children and realized that everything was actually fine.

2. You have friends in kindergarten

You don't always have to work hard to build the kids' social life. Swamping them with playdates sometimes serves only to calm you (or stress you). Listen to your kids and to what they really need, and if you have a kid who doesn't feel like having friends over or going to a friend's every day or two, remember that he comes back home to you after he's worked a day with all these little people. And you don't feel like having the secretary or your business partner or colleague over after work every day, do you? Give it a break—they spend the whole day with their friends.

3. You do know

Who said that if your neighbor is thrilled about a new and innovative educational method that she used on her son to help him sleep alone at night and you don't feel compelled to try it, this makes you a bad parent? Parent counselors and advisers are always there, and you don't always need them.

4. Stay out of it

Despite the noise, the fighting, the jealousy, the rivalry—siblings are the best present you can give your children. They form the social field that teaches your child the most, basically because they always stick around and especially when you stay out of it.

5. Let them help

Kids need to feel useful in order to develop. Children's usefulness can be physical (folding socks) or emotional (letting you rest). Let them contribute, because there is no better or more significant feeling. Remember that you are damaging them when you spoil them while depriving them of a sense of significance. Children who can't find significance in being useful, independent, and helpful will find it in a sense of deprivation, spoiled behavior, or being uncooperative.

6. Don't answer, listen

We usually pretend to listen. What can we do in a daily routine that includes hundreds of sentences that begin with "Mom . . ."? We create automatic responses like, "Really?" "That's great!" "You don't say?" while browsing through Facebook and clicking Like on a post of someone we don't really know. When we get around to listening, we often quickly move on to advising, scolding, or giving them a piece of our mind. But listening is sometimes just listening. All they need is someone to listen and give them a Like.

7. Relationships are more important than school

School is important, but not important enough to ruin your relationship. Don't forget that, the next time you try to help them with homework they're having trouble understanding and lose your temper, or when you threaten that if they don't get their homework done they'll be punished, or when you're angry with them after a PTA meeting or let them know how disappointed you are. Your hope of fixing them or educating them to have academic interest isn't necessarily worth the high price you might pay. Sometimes, it has the exact opposite result *and* damages your relationship in the process.

8. Don't brand them

Screening tests are excellent tools, but after it's over you go back home with the exact same child you left with. The fact that you now know that he has ADD, learning disabilities, autism, regulation issues, or emotional difficulties doesn't mean someone has swapped your child. He's wonderful and marvelous and now it has a name, but don't forget the name you gave him when you carried him out of the hospital in his baby seat. That's his real name.

9. Give them five minutes

Quality time isn't taking a day off to be with them or buying them a ton of things. It can be a five-minute chat in the bath or seven minutes under the blanket with a flashlight or driving in the car or watching a terrible TV series they love, diving into it with them and realizing that it's not that bad after all. Quality time isn't measured by time but by quality.

10. Spare yourselves the comparisons

Examining other people's children reflects nothing but your guilt feelings or, alternatively, your sense of superiority. Forget about what you think you're seeing—no one has it easy, and the fact that their child behaves well at the dining table or occupies herself, says thank you, or sleeps through the night doesn't mean that those parents aren't experiencing difficulties in places where you're finding it easy. So let go of the comparisons, because at least half of the time they're misleading you.

11. Don't suffer

Don't do things that you hate doing with your kids. The good parent isn't necessarily the one who does arts and crafts every day with his child or visits the playground; they're not the one who works on fine motor skills or plays plenty of classical music. The good parent is the one who takes the time to do something fun with the kids.

12. It's okay if they get angry

Don't be alarmed by a discontented child. Don't think that you are bad parents just because your child is angry or frustrated right now. Happy children aren't children whose every need has been met, but ones who saw happy parents, ones who managed to overcome difficulties, who learned to see the full half of the glass (and you need an empty half to do that).

13. Your criticism will destroy them

Their self-image is their fuel tank for life, and you're in charge of it. I've never yet met a happy person who had low self-esteem. So every time you criticize or judge them, think hard whether you really want to play a role that only contributes to a tendency to judge and criticize themselves. Their whole lives. Your criticism isn't worth the toll it takes. It's worth nothing if she's pretty but doesn't feel pretty, if she's smart but doesn't believe in her own intelligence, if she made the effort of getting a high grade but isn't pleased with it. Every time you choose to see what is lacking, you take fuel out of their tanks. Every time you see what there is, even if it's not as glorious as it could be, you'll see their fuel tank refill.

14. Reinforce their weaker qualities

We tend to praise our children mainly for the qualities that are the most glorious, the ones they naturally possess, neglecting the qualities that need the positive feedback most of all. This is where the greatest and most significant job of encouragement comes into play. It's with the child we singled out as less responsible, the girl who's less patient, the boy who's less flexible that we have the duty of searching for the hidden quality and being more excited by it than by the qualities that come naturally; we must give it a name, show them that they are in the middle of a process, and the bigger and stronger they get, the greater this quality will become.

And in the family, even when it's very tempting to ask the responsible child to watch over his little brother or the pasta boiling on the stove and to ask the child who draws best to make a greeting card for Grandma, switch their roles around once in a while. Let them practice in a safe environment the quality that still isn't available to them on the outside. When the less-responsible child hears that you're counting on him and that without the responsibility he showed you wouldn't have managed to eat such tasty pasta, see what happens to him on the inside (and sometimes on the outside too).

15. A bit of humility

One of the greatest challenges that faces every parent is the challenge of humility: the realization that even if we think a certain

problem has a clear solution and a certain behavior only one logical interpretation, our way isn't necessarily the right way—not
because we're not right, but because we're raising a person who
is different from us, who has different limitations, different emotions and experiences.

All our children are different from us—they have their own
personality, temperament, character—but the child who brings
us face-to-face with completely opposite qualities, who supposedly behaves in a way that contradicts the deep values our per-
sonalities are based on, is the most complex when we talk of the
challenge of humility. It's particularly with her that we need to
know a little less and ask a little more.

Otherwise, we belittle her, distrust her, disregard our differences. And she'll always know better what's right for herself.

16. You're not just a parent

In the first year, your baby almost always meets only the parent
in you. This is the time you're supposed to satisfy all the baby's
needs and give up on many of your own needs. But the older they
get, remember that they have to see you as a human being: to see
you failing, happy, sad, tired, enjoying an activity that isn't related
to them, hungry, frustrated, being a couple, talking with friends,
and finding satisfaction in work. They need mainly to understand
that we aren't perfect either, because parents who don't expose
imperfection raise children who are anxious about their own imperfection. And children who don't see their parents enjoying
their relationship or work or grown-ups' fun feel betrayed when
they see that the world outside doesn't always revolve around
them. Let them encounter you and trust them to handle it.

17. Laugh more

A little research I conducted over more than a decade of meeting with children and adolescents raises one of the saddest expressions children say about us adults—that we almost never laugh. Do yourself a favor—laugh.

18. Be grateful for what you have

On the next family trip, put the tensions and the thoughts about what you left at home aside for a moment, raise your head from your cell, and look in the backseat for a second. Look at each and every one of them, because very soon they'll be in a car of their own with a family of their own. Be thankful for what you have, remember what a privilege it is for a whole family to drive in a car together, pat yourselves on the back because it's hard being parents, play a happy song, and pray that someone up there watches over you.

As simple as that.

fifty-two

A Word of Encouragement

SOMETIMES, WHEN I THINK ABOUT MY MOTHER, I'M overcome by a sense of sadness and missed opportunity. I imagine her feeling deeply regretful about things she would have wanted to say to me but didn't, about moments she would have wanted to be there for me but couldn't, for not having told me enough how much she loves me and how proud she is of the person I've become. I imagine her looking back on situations from day-to-day life and regretting choosing to criticize instead of clarify, imagine her sitting up there and suddenly realizing that what really counts in the end are the moments when we hugged enough, loved enough, got excited enough, said enough words of encouragement.

For my part, I'm sorry for being angry at her and at the illness that she brought into my world. I'm sorry I didn't tell her what a wonderful mother she was, how dear she was to me, that I knew it was almost more than she could bear to know that the time of our love was running out, that I didn't tell her how amazingly she coped with the dwindling time we had and was still always there, happy and optimistic. I'm sorry I didn't tell her what an amazing woman she is, that I concentrated on myself and not on her or us.

Being an orphan, beyond the sense of lack or longing it brings, is composed of all the things we didn't manage to do. True enough, life is always too short; we live and go on completing our "unfinished" business, but there are some things that it's important to pause for. "Unfinished" things will remain after us, carried in our children's souls, making up their self-image. Because never mind psychologists, parent counselors, medication, pedagogical methods, punishments, prizes, research, practice, achievements, and other important and less or more effective tools—ultimately, what matters most is saying enough words of encouragement. To me, this is the most significant parental task.

We make the mistake of thinking that educating children means fixing them, marking boundaries for them, being authoritative, explaining things they don't understand. This is the childhood experience we grew up with, and this is the classic parental figure—authoritative, efficient, containing. The encouraging parent is perceived as somewhat lax, overenthusiastic. But through the language of encouragement you can pass on deep educational and emotional messages that you can't pass on in any other language, certainly not one of criticism or humiliation. I can tell my children what I think about people who give up on themselves, who don't know how to be a good friend, or who regard authority with contempt, but I'll never put them in those categories. Children do a great job of learning from the model they see, the philosophical conversations, the debates we have with them. From criticism directed toward them, they only learn to criticize themselves. They learn only that they aren't good enough. And so, every time you criticize your children, you're missing out, getting confused. You think you're educating them, but you're not.

In the contract between us and the kids, we need to include a term that specifies that no matter what happens or how bad they mess up, we'll always see the good and encourage it, focus the flashlight on it. And when it comes to the discordant, difficult places, we won't make too much of them. Not because they don't interest us, but because in our children's inner protocol, what should register is the following memory: "In our house, everyone always believed in me. Even if I didn't succeed, my parents didn't lose faith, didn't push the dagger in deeper, always saw the best of things. And through that small goodness that they saw and encouraged, I could see the goodness in myself, could understand that it's more worthwhile to make an effort to create goodness and receive enthusiasm, appreciation, and respect in return than to create badness and receive . . . nothing." Yes, just that, nothing.

If children do not feel significant in their own home, then when they refuse to cooperate ("Every morning I have to beg you to get ready"), don't do their homework ("Do you have homework? When are you going to do your homework? Do you need help with your homework?"), or misbehave ("Go to your room." "Say sorry." "We'll talk about this in the evening." "You'll be punished for this.") and that's what we focus on, they mistakenly conclude that that's what they are—uncooperative, that that's the only way they belong in the family, that that's the part they play. If that's how they gain significance, why, then, should they stop? Why should they give up that place? What are you offering them in exchange for them to claim a different role? Because when they calm down after the tantrum, no one praises them and says: "You're a child who knows how to calm himself. It's amazing how you overcame your frustration." But in the midst of the tantrum? Oh my, the concentration, the attention, the significance.

Yes, it's hard to put in a good word when it seems as if there's nothing to praise. But you know what? There always is. You have to really search for it, bite your tongue and take the chance of feeling slightly embarrassed, because we're not practiced in saying positive things. But imagine that this is your last day, God forbid, remember that what you put into their consciousness will accompany them for life, and realize that your view of them and your faith in them—those are what will help them create a new reality when things get hard.

The relatively easy part of the task is when the children manage to create a bottom line that is worthy of encouragement in your eyes: She's been crying the whole month when saying goodbye at kindergarten, and, here, a day without crying. Natu rally, we'll encourage her, raise a toast to her in the evening, call Grandma. But what about all those days she cried and you tried everything (telling her it makes you sad, saying that it's time to say goodbye, offering rewards, being authoritative)? Did you just manage to contain the hardship she experienced in saying goodbye by not saying much, understanding, and then searching for the points where she cried less? Or maybe cried less loudly? Or only at the entrance to the kindergarten and not all the way from home? Maybe a time she was soothed more easily? There, in the hardest place for you, when she's still not offering the bottom line that will mark the fact that you've reached the destination, there, with the little that there is, you should get excited, ask her how she managed to do it, tell her that it's amazing and that it will get better each day, that it's okay to cry, but, wow, she's overcoming it so well. It's in the places that you're having the hardest time with them that you should use the tool of encouragement. And when you do it, believe me—parental authority will seem like child's play.

The idea is not to say "you're amazing" or "light of my life" or "you're the most beautiful child" or "the smartest kid." Your words of encouragement seep deeper the more focused they are. Your words have to meet your children genuinely, at a concrete moment, not necessarily when they are at their best but when they're creating something good. Imagine your mother coming for a visit, seeing the children, and whispering in your ear: "I love you." Feels good, right? And now imagine her seeing you making supper, talking to the children, and then whispering to you: "You're such a wonderful mother. Your patience amazes me. Your ability to contain everyone's quirks, stay positive, and get everything done is really rare." Or imagine your father stopping by for a visit and instead of slapping you on the shoulder with the customary manly gesture, stopping and saying: "Listen, you are quite the father! You're so present, so significant in the children's lives. It's a pleasure seeing you spend so much time with them. I missed out on that when you were kids."

Your words don't have to be the "most" and you don't need to add big superlatives, even though these do make a person feel good and are heartwarming. The precise words are the ones that reach the roots, strengthen the trunk, and let children attribute to themselves the wonderful qualities that exist in them. And don't be alarmed if your plant hasn't yet blossomed. Remember that the water you offer in the form of encouraging words give it life and that your job is to water it.

And no, there's no such thing as overdoing it. When what you say is accurate, little seedlings soak it into their ground, and when it gets tough outside—and it always gets tough outside—they will turn to that good earth and remember that they know how to overcome, find solutions, turn a new page, wait patiently, not despair, be generous, be responsible, and many other qualities that are all in them. And how will they know that they're there if the people closest to them don't see them or tell them about them, aren't moved by them? They know it if you say it. Only if you say it. You'll never hear a grown person say: "My parents? They didn't judge me, didn't criticize me, but accepted me just the way I am, loved me unconditionally, encouraged me, had faith in me, always saw the things that worked, and that's what screwed me up and ruined my life." The things we really regret are always the things we didn't say, the moments we missed out on because we were preoccupied or focused on what wasn't working well or used painful words to express our good intention.

Our ability to know all that is good in our children and to tell them about it starts with our willingness to accept the fact that they aren't perfect, just like we aren't. But words of encouragement are like a prophecy that fulfills itself, just as despairing words are. Say words of force and they will use words of force; say words of criticism and they'll use words of criticism; say words of discontentment and frustration and these will be their inner words; say words of accusation and they'll learn to accuse; say words of faith and they will believe; say words of understanding and they will know understanding; say words of encouragement and they'll know how to encourage themselves; say words of closeness and they'll know how to get closer and feel close; say words of forgiveness and they'll know it's okay to say sorry and be imperfect.

fifty-three

For Eight Years I Talked to a Child Who Looked Away

H E WAS TWO YEARS, EIGHT MONTHS, AND FOUR DAYS old. On the morning of October 4, we had an appointment at the Center for Child Development. I got the bag ready the night before, not forgetting wipes, a bottle of water in case he got thirsty, a game he liked to play in the car, some cookies in a bag. Packing the bag gave me some relief, as if I was packing myself a bag of hopes for tomorrow. I wish you could just pack to prepare for this life, I thought. I hope the evaluator will laugh about what an anxious mother I am, say what a wonderful child he is and that we came for nothing. I hope we will share the cookies on the way back home and I'll call Yuval, who'll be in a meeting at work, and he'll answer and we'll both breathe a sigh of relief. I put in the pack of cigarettes I kept in the kitchen drawer for special occasions, but I couldn't find a lighter. And then the sense of helplessness began to seep in.

The way back home was strange. I buckled him in, my beautiful boy, started the old Mitsubishi car that had just come out of the garage, and played him the song he liked over and over and over again, just the way he liked it. My heart was pounding. I vaguely remembered what I would remember in great detail as time passed: something about a spectrum, something about a lot of support we'll need in order to cope. I didn't talk to him as I usually did. I thought about all the times in the car I used to sing to him, try to make him laugh, make animal noises, ask questions that were never answered. Now I couldn't even look at him through the mirror; it was too painful. Yuval texted me twice while we were at the center. I didn't reply. What a shame you can't take kids to the garage, I thought, how sad is it to have a broken child without a garage to fix him.

I found myself parked outside Yuval's office and I texted him: "I'm downstairs." I made sure the air conditioner was on and the song was playing over again and waited for my husband outside the car with a cigarette in my hand, no light. He came down quickly, and his worried expression made it even more painful. He didn't ask any questions, just hugged me. I burst into tears. I cried for myself, for him, for the perfect child we had in the morning, who was now gone. I cried from a place that was new and unfamiliar to me—I was crying from my womb.

Two months later, and we still hadn't told anyone. We weren't ready to face the world. I knew the stories told with compassion and pity about that woman's daughter and those people's son— ADD, regulation issues, emotional issues, autism, allergies, mental problems, delayed development, language problems. Now people would look at me like that. I failed at creating an undamaged child that I could flaunt.

I knew I couldn't get confused, I couldn't be that broken woman outside the Mitsubishi. I knew that I had come back home with the same child I had left with that morning—that he was mine, ours, that we knew and loved him more than anything in the whole world. But now I had to deal with a title someone had stuck to him, and yes, at first, all I could see when I looked at him was that title.

There was no day or night, all the days became glued together and turned into months.

And there was only deadly fear, frustration, a sense of failure. It takes time to realize who you are in your own story when someone suddenly changes the title, gives away the ending, and it's not a happy one. We'd only just got started—how could it be that one day, at the age of two years and eight months, someone already wrote the ending for us?

One evening, after he was asleep, I sat on the balcony, took a deep breath, and remembered that this was my child. Long before any word or definition in any medical guidebook, this was my baby. I realized that the way I see him would be what dictates his way; it would be what sets him on his path and stays in him when he sets out in the world. I realized that I was his garage, and I may not be able to totally fix him, but I can accept him, help him improve, be his gas station, be proud of him, not ashamed, and fight for him like I've never fought before. And every time things get too hard, I step out onto the balcony and remember that I'm the most important thing in his life, that I'm the sky above him and the ground beneath his feet. I was ready for the battle of my life, of our life. I was ready to tell the world about my beloved boy.

I'm not sure when the word *autistic* was said explicitly. It always hurts as much as it did the first time I heard it. And when you think about it, how can one word define so many difficulties, so many nuances? It always felt like a great injustice to fit it all into one corner with one title.

We told him he was autistic during a conversation about a particular hardship, trying to make him understand that it's not his fault, that there's a reason why he feels that it's harder for him than it is for everyone else. Later on, every difficulty was given a separate talk, a separate love, a separate encouragement, because how do you encourage an autistic child? It's simpler to encourage understanding of a situation, talk about fear of change, about the courage it takes to step out of your room when someone has changed the living room sofa and it's suddenly not the same living room, about being angry with yourself when you don't manage to overcome the challenges. When you talk without titles and without fear, the "autistic" becomes less relevant.

When our baby celebrated his sixteenth birthday, I stood on that same balcony with him. I told him I was so proud of the progress he was making, of the way he deals with his difficulty and doesn't give up. I told him that if, when he was just three, anyone had told me that at sixteen he would speak with me, sometimes even look me in the eye, be so clever, go to a normal school with an integration assistant, and not be ashamed of who he is, if someone had told me that all the love his father and I would give him would nurture confidence and happiness and a will to do better every day anew, then that day he was sitting there in the car seat in the Mitsubishi, I would have been much less worried.

I told him that when he was three and I was told he was autistic, I was sad, and that today, too, sometimes, when he's having a hard time, when he's angry with himself for not understanding the rules of this world, the words and expressions, when he worries about how he'll find love and how he'll know if a girl in his class is or isn't interested, I remember that sadness of when he was three. But then I think that it's not as sad as it was then, because throughout the years he taught me to believe in him, taught me what encourages him and what calms him and even how he manages to learn new things. I just listened to him all these years, because he's a wonderful teacher.

I didn't tell him how many nights I'd stand on that balcony and curse the stars, how many evenings I felt as if I had no more strength for anything, not for believing in him, feeling sorry for him, feeling sorry for myself, listening to specialists with bleak prognoses, teaching new learning assistants what he needs, containing his tantrums, no energy to argue with Yuval about what he can and should demand of him or can't and should do for him, protect him from mean children, cry with him about not having any friends, stay at home with him while kids his age kissed and danced in clubs, go with him to new places and see how difficult it is for him. The heavens witnessed my most secret prayers: *Please just give him one friend; please let him know how to shower himself; please let him express what he feels instead of hurting himself; please let him make less strange noises, let him get a joke, know how to ride a bike, survive a class trip, not think that if someone is shouting a mile away, he's shouting at him. Please let us have enough money to take on this impossible mission and give him everything he needs. Please, please, please.*

Before I went in with him to sit down to the celebratory dinner we had prepared for his birthday, I asked him if he'd be offended if I took a few more minutes alone on the balcony. He laughed and said: "Mom, nothing you do can offend me," and closed the glass door behind him. I took a deep breath and thought a festive thought in honor of his birthday. I thought that everything pays off in the end. That maybe we were lucky, because the experts who saw him announced with confidence that he would never be independent, never be able to learn in a normal framework, maybe wouldn't even talk or communicate. They told me to prepare myself for a child who would be detached from the world. But I knew in the deepest sense of the word that it wasn't just luck, it was unbelievably hard work.

I remembered how he had learned to make eye contact when he was eight. For eight years I talked to a child who looked away. I never saw his expression. One day, while we were standing in the kitchen, I passed him the cottage cheese to put on the table (I insisted he help every day), and he looked at me completely by accident. I grabbed his face with both hands in excitement and said in a trembling voice: "That's it! You've done it! You're looking me in the eye! I've got a child who can look me in the eye! Daddy, come look what just happened here. You did it! You did it! We did it! We did it!" And I started dancing this funny dance in the kitchen and he laughed and got excited along with us.

We decided to leave the behavioral specialist who had accompanied us for six months and believed in a stern approach, charts, rewards, and punishments. I knew it worked very well for others, but deep inside I felt from the very start that it wasn't right for our family. I knew that with my child only happiness and excitement would revive dormant places, teach what is right, emphasize the things that work. And so, for two years, every time he looked us in the eye, we celebrated him—the look, the achievement—and when he chose to look away, we said nothing. And gradually, the good seeped in, the happiness prevailed, and we looked at each other more and were impressed by him every time anew.

At the end of the day, every day, I had to remind myself that I wasn't the issue. He's not the terrible thing that happened to me. The issue is not dwelling on what I could do, the mistakes I made, or how poor we were. At the end of each day, I had to force myself to disconnect from the fears and the guilt, from the demons and the bleak forecasts, to find the good, believe in the next day, be happy, see in this terrible difficulty an opportunity to become better. Yes, therapists are important, so are good frameworks and specialists, but there is no cure like faith, no treatment like constantly seeing what's working and working with it, even when most things aren't working. The daily task is to find the things that work, identify the buds of progress even before they bud, and you can do that only when you remember and show thanks every day for what there is.

Today I have a different kid. A little strange at times, incredibly cool, funny, clever, a boy who loves people and still has to practice every new situation fifty times in order to catalog it in his manual, to feel he's succeeding. Behind me there are dark days of despair, frustration, and plenty of fear; before me are many more years of hard work; and above me a beautiful sky full of stars that are sometimes a little hard to see, but they're there.

fifty-four

"What, My Love?"

AND WHAT IF MY WHOLE APPROACH, MY PERSPECTIVES and the way they're translated into daily reality, what if it's all just one big mistake? Could it be that the overawareness is only there to serve my unwillingness or inability to be authoritative? Maybe this aspiration to understand the children's language of the heart is actually an obstruction? Maybe everything is supposed to look completely different—clear, with more exclamation marks and as few questions and misgivings as possible? Maybe this whole experiment in humanism doesn't work properly in a family unit, where there should be parents, rules, and children?

I wish you could educate a child using one method, and then take a second shot with another method. Take Yoav, for example, my second son. Let's say that with the first difficulty he encountered at school, at the age of seven, I'd taken him for a checkup and had sat to do homework with him every day. Like it or not— he would learn to read, he would learn English, he would learn to be organized. Yes, we'd fight on the way and he would cry with frustration, feel misunderstood, hate himself and me, and together we would struggle against this inferiority inherited from god knows who, but by the third grade he would catch up. And when he would refuse to read books, I'd make him, just like I made him buckle his seatbelt, because it's important in my eyes, because he'd thank me in the end, and who needs an illiterate child? So I'd fight the disability and, in the process, inevitably fight him too. Hopefully, he would show less and less resistance, and gradually become more educated, grow, and give in to the system according to which I know what's best for him and he, he just needs to be a good soldier, because it's for his own good, because it will pay off in the end.

Generally speaking, there are some days when I feel as if it could be wonderful to raise good soldiers, especially with the chaos of five children, five souls with their separate wants, desires, complex characters, and immediate needs that collide every day, every hour with my own needs and the needs of the other family members.

So in the second go with that beloved child, we'd go back to second grade. The teacher would alert us, the empty notebooks would speak for themselves, but I'd tell myself and his father, "Wait, let's give him some time." Because when I did sit down to do homework with him, on the few days he would remember and I would be impressed by how responsible he was, he would understand. "So maybe we can help with a bit of corrective instruction," I'd tell his father. "But let's give him time, find out together what subject he's good at, where he has a spark of success or talent and start from there." The teacher wouldn't be too pleased in the meantime, but at least we wouldn't give him the feeling that he's flawed.

Even after the screening test in the third grade, when we came to realize that there were lots of "issues," we wouldn't confront him, wouldn't force him or fight with him. We would recognize that he's good at math and start reinforcing him there. He'd get private lessons in mathematics. We would turn a blind eye when he'd fail the other subjects and work with what there was. When he grew up a little, we would start having conversations with him about our expectations as parents, his frustrations, what we would define for him as success. We would reach agreements according to which he would make an effort and we would help where things got hard. We wouldn't make him doubt his own abilities, not for one second, but mark out small objectives and encourage him as he climbed.

No, this story doesn't end with a child who made it to the top, or with a TED Talk about how to overcome learning disabilities in amicable ways. Today I have a child going into high school who still struggles every day with basic learning tasks that his twelve-year-old sister could do when she was still in the womb. But he's good at math. Really good. And the teachers are happy with him even though they think (and say), "Too bad, if he worked a little harder he would come closer to realizing his potential, but it's great that he participates in class. It's so interesting to hear his opinions about pedagogical issues." His notebooks are still empty, his and our frustration is still there, and when they give out the report cards, we focus on the kind words every homeroom teacher writes about him and his grade in math.

On the days when the disturbing messages about the importance of success at school aren't humming in my ears, I thank

God for not pushing, for choosing as parents not to trample all over this wonderful child in the name of one form of success or another. Because we gained a happy child, a child who fully trusts us, who is willing to share with us all the most difficult feelings and uncertainties he has with himself and with life. We gained a child who has peace, peace from unrealistic expectations, criticism, the difficult feelings that exist in any child with learning disabilities, which with time become the disability itself. We gained a child who might fail high school, but I have no doubt that he will succeed in life.

Doubt comes at the more difficult moments, the moments when life gets the better of me, when I'm exhausted, tired of maintaining the mechanism that sees only the good and what there is. In moments like these, I ask myself if I haven't made a mistake. Maybe if I'd made the adolescent go to ballet when she decided to give it up, she wouldn't be sitting around and moping about how bored she is, what a hard time she's having socially, or how terrible she looks? Maybe if I'd listened less or understood her need to leave less, and just knew that it was good for her, that we don't quit in our house, that going to ballet classes is important, that even if I have to drag her over there myself she's going, no matter what—maybe then I wouldn't have to confront such hard questions in her most difficult places? Maybe at this point, in the other scenario, she would be on her way to ballet, dealing with all the muck out there, busier and less available for the muck she has with herself and with me?

And what if the first time my kids were cheeky at a young age they got a mouthful, got scared, gained a profound realization that in our house you respect parents and are not cheeky, even when you're angry? You don't say "dummy" at four, "I hate you" at six, or "Get out of the room" at twelve, and you certainly don't contemptuously imitate me behind my back at fifteen? Maybe if he had gotten an assertive mouthful, I wouldn't be stuck with this child, who does speak to me very respectfully most of the time but also gets totally confused when he's angry? Because what mom—never mind mom, parents' counselor!—who has been chanting the most humanistic methods for raising children for seventeen years would want to be caught with children who speak to her disrespectfully? What parents' counselor would want to be caught with children who are lacking in motivation, a social spark, children who don't align with the parent when she finally does decide to be authoritative but who talk back, argue, nurture a personality, make a mess, get angry and bored, refuse to help, think only of themselves, have a hard time, get banged against the walls of life, take one step forward and two steps back, two forward and one back?

But in this negative stream of consciousness, which is so unlike me, I'm committed to remind myself that these kids of mine, the ones who fail and embarrass, annoy and laze about, avoid and give up, are the most wonderful people there are. They are funny, independent; they help each other when they're not fighting; they help out at home when it works out; they contribute and are useful in their own way in every framework they are part of. They are good people, sensitive to others, understanding of the weak; they look out for themselves and share their thoughts with the world. They know how to express their emotions and understand others' emotions, know how to be happy and make others happy, know how to love. The ability to see them this way really depends on the day, the time, my emotional state, but mainly it depends on the understanding that just as we, the grown-ups in their lives, aren't perfect, so, too, they are far from perfection, and that raising a person is something that takes time. And yes, even when it comes to a parents' counselor who accompanies families through the most wondrous process there is—weaving a relationship with their children—even for her it doesn't always work, and she doesn't wake up every morning in a tidy house with polite kids and classical music playing in the background.

I get up every morning to work at the toughest job there is—being a parent. Not being right or dignified, not even appreciated. And it's just when I'm most uncertain about my path that suddenly one of my children calls me from another room, and I answer "What, my love?" and it reminds me that, in the end, that's the whole story.